THE
BARGAIN HUNTER'S
GUIDE TO
USED FURNITURE

THE
BARGAIN HUNTER'S
GUIDE TO
USED
FURNITURE

THOMAS M. VOSS

A Delta Book

A Delta Book

Published by
Dell Publishing Co., Inc.
1 Dag Hammarskjold Plaza
New York, New York 10017

Copyright © 1980 by Thomas M. Voss

Printed in the United States of America
First printing—April 1980

Book Design by Elaine Golt Gongora

LIBRARY OF CONGRESS CATALOGING IN PUBLICATION DATA

Voss, Thomas M 1945–
The bargain hunter's guide to used furniture.

(A Delta book)
Bibliography: p. 163
Includes index.
1. Furniture, used. I. Title.
TS885.V67   645'.4   79–25563

ISBN: 0–440–50464–3

Also by
Thomas M. Voss
Antique American Country Furniture:
Americana at Auction
A Field Guide

CONTENTS

Acknowledgments

I am indebted to the following individuals and shops for their invaluable assistance in the preparation of this book: Almost Antiques, Manayunk, Pennsylvania; Art's Resale, Clinton, New Jersey; As Time Goes By, New Hope, Pennsylvania; Billy Carrier at the Golden Nugget, Lambertville, New Jersey; Nondas Case, Nina Cosintino, Elliott Hulick, Lina B. Knight, Mat and Pat McKeown, Sara Scully, and Marie and Joan Tucker at the Tomato Factory, Hopewell, New Jersey; Greenbranch Antiques, Lambertville, New Jersey; Clyde Neville at the Whitehouse Manor Antique Center, Whitehouse, New Jersey; Al Novello, Fleetwood, Pennsylvania; Piper Second Hand, Pipersville, Pennsylvania; Plumsteadville Village Antiques, Plumstead, Pennsylvania; The Porkyard, Lambertville, New Jersey; Wayne Pratt, Marlboro, Massachusetts; and Betty and Oto Ramirez, Middletown, New York.

I am also grateful to the following furniture companies for providing me with photographs and information: Baker Furniture Company; Bassett Furniture Industries; Brady Furniture Company; Broyhill Furniture Industries; Burris Industries; Century Furniture Company; Davis Cabinet Company; Gunlocke Company; Henredon Furniture Industries; John Widdicomb Company; Karges Furniture Company; Kemp Furniture Industries; Lane Company; Riverside Furniture Company; Sligh Furniture Company; Stanley Furniture Company; and Winterhouse Furniture Company.

My special thanks go to Mimi Jones for thinking of me before I thought of myself and to Bob and Elaine Lutz for the "use of the hall."

THE NEWS
IS USED:
AN INTRODUCTION

THIS IS A BOOK for people who want to live tastefully but not wastefully. And today one of the best ways to do that is to get in on the used-furniture boom.

Did you know that, according to some reliable estimates, more used furniture than new is currently being purchased in this country? Did you know that some dealers are actually hauling truckloads of used furniture from one part of the country to another just to meet the demand? There's an "Old Rush" going on out there, and this book will show you how to become a "prospector."

At this point you may be asking yourself what exactly I mean by "used furniture." For the purposes of this book, it is furniture that was mass produced in American factories from about 1870 to 1960. None of it is yet considered antique, but certain pieces that are particularly fine examples of their period or style, like certain models of automobiles, have become "classics." Within this relatively short span of about ninety years a multitude of styles were produced: Eastlake, Mission, Art Nouveau, Golden Oak, Baronial, Art Deco, Depression Modern, and Swedish Modern, to name most of them and not to mention such specialty items as wicker, metal, bentwood, and horn furniture. Moreover, within each of those categories, hundreds and sometimes thousands of variations of each style were manufactured. Today all of them are being sought and bought so enthusiastically that not long ago a major New York television station featured a five-day series of news reports titled *The Used Boom.*

Many factors fuel the fires of the used-furniture market: nostalgia, the search for "good" goods, the powerful appeal of earlier designs that are no longer made, and the satisfaction to be gained from do-it-yourself repairing and refinishing, among others. But perhaps the most important factor is the financial one. Today even the blandest, most boring new furniture represents a sizable investment. And the moment you buy your brand-new hundred-dollar chair, for example, it becomes a piece of used furniture. Depreciation erodes its value so quickly that you'd probably be lucky to get twenty-five dollars for it in a garage sale. And of course as inflation takes its toll, new furniture will become even more expensive.

On the other hand, used furniture made between 1870 and 1960 often costs far less than new furniture, and it usually appreciates in value. The very desirable pieces, in fact, go up in value faster than the rate of inflation, so it's little wonder that the used-furniture market is strong and getting stronger.

Unfortunately, though, many buyers of used furniture are vulnerable to being cheated in the marketplace because they've cheated themselves out of a solid understanding of what they're buying. They've never made the effort to learn the difference between good furniture and bad. They have only a hazy notion of when the used furniture they've bought was made, let alone why or where or how. And that's a shame, because the knowledge and information necessary to buy used furniture wisely is not difficult to acquire, and having that knowledge increases one's enjoyment of the furniture tremendously. Furthermore, without that knowledge, the probability of getting a bargain in used furniture *decreases* tremendously. It's like playing a game without knowing the rules or the strategy: the only way you're going to win—or get a bargain—is by sheer luck.

But it takes a lot more than luck to ferret out bargains in used furniture, and if you're intrigued with the question of how to do it, then this book is for you. Part One not only gives you the facts about where and how to buy used furniture (including some strategies and places you may never have thought of) but also tells you the all-important inside story on quality in furniture woods, construction, ornamentation, and finishes. Part Two details the realistic possibilities of repairing, reviving, and refinishing used furniture: money-saving tips on how to do it yourself, or when to let an expert do it for you, or when it may not be worth doing at all. In Part Three, the entire array of ninety years of used furniture is laid out for you, including both the historical backgrounds of the various styles and information on the current market in those styles.

In this *Bargain Hunter's Guide* you'll discover such things as why the design, construction, and general condition of a piece of used furniture may be far more important than its age; how mass production accounted for as much attractive and well-made furniture as tasteless and shoddy furniture; why certain pieces of used furniture will not grow in value, and which pieces will; how to avoid being cheated and deceived; how to find bargains; and even how to bargain for bargains. For my purpose in writing this book was not only to help you follow your nose but also your "knows," and I hope you enjoy reading it as much as I've enjoyed writing it for you.

THE
BARGAIN HUNTER'S
GUIDE TO
USED FURNITURE

PART ONE

1

GETTING
USED TO YOU:
WHERE AND HOW TO BUY

IF YOU HAVE enough money, you can spend it freely to buy
anything you want, anytime you want. Conversely, if you
have enough time, you can spend it freely in hunting for
what you want at the right price. But if you're like me,
and most of the other bargain hunters I know, you fall
somewhere in between: You have a little money, and a
little time, but you never have enough of both. And that's
precisely what this chapter is about—where and how to
spend your precious time and money, and spend them
wisely, in the vast marketplace for used furniture.

The Marketplace

Everyone knows what a bargain is: It's an item that's
priced below its current market value. In the conventional
business world, the market value might be considered the
retail price. Anything that costs less than that price may
be a bargain; anything that costs a lot less is definitely a
bargain. Regulations against price fixing, and competition
among manufacturers and retailers, are what fuel the bargain machine, and comparative shoppers reap the be-
nefits.

But the used-furniture marketplace is anything but
conventional. For one thing, it's unregulated. For another,
there are no true wholesale and retail markets. Prices can
vary wildly from one shop or auction to the next, and
from one geographical area to the next. Golden Oak furniture may cost ten times as much on the West Coast as
on the East. Depression Modern furniture may be worth-
less in the country and valuable in the city.

The point is that in order to know whether or not you're getting a bargain in used furniture, you've got to get your feet wet in the marketplace, and basically there are two ways to do this. The easiest way is to buy price guides to the things that interest you, and there are many versions of price guides ranging from inexpensive paperback books to magazine-style periodicals. Unfortunately, however, there are many pitfalls inherent in price guides. First, any published price is obsolete the moment it's published; second, you usually cannot determine whether a published price is a "bid price" or an "asked price," that is, at what point in the range of prices from highest to lowest the published price falls; and third, you almost never know the condition of the piece or what it really looked like, both of which can significantly influence the price of an object.

For the bargain hunter, therefore, the best way to become familiar with current prices is a little reality therapy. In other words, you should visit as many places as possible where used furniture is sold and make notes— mental or otherwise—about the prices of comparable objects without necessarily having an intention of buying anything. In this way you can get your feet wet in the marketplace without getting cold feet about making a mistake on your first purchase. In addition, you might want to visit a few retail and discount stores that sell *new* furniture. That will give you an idea of just how expensive it is and may motivate you to continue your personal market-survey of used furniture.

Some places are better than others for making price comparisons and often for getting bargains. Here are a few that I think are particularly profitable to visit:

- Auctions
- Antiques shows
- Open-air flea markets that cater to transient dealers
- Thrift shops
- Garage sales
- A dealer's shop that *does not* specialize in what you're looking for

Figure 1
A country antiques auction in New Hampshire. The auctioneer is flanked by his "spotters," keeping an eagle-eye out for bids from the audience.

• A dealer's shop that sells what you're looking for but that is located in an area where there are several other dealers who do not sell what you want

In the following pages I'll expand on these thoughts as I go over the various advantages and disadvantages of each source for used furniture, as well as how to bargain for it. I'll also have a few final words of wisdom.

Auctions

Three's a crowd. It's also the minimum number of people required for an auction: two bidders and an auctioneer. In fact, during the bidding for any particular item, every auction eventually resolves itself into those three people —the high bidder, who wins the item; the underbidder, who loses it; and the auctioneer, who takes the money.

But that's a simplification, of course, since every auction starts with more than two bidders, and that causes complications. For example, even if you've never attended an auction, you've probably heard of auction fever—a contagious disease that can grip an auction audience and cause it to lose self-control, bidding higher and higher for no apparent reason. The disease strikes the amateur and the professional alike, and only those with ice in their veins are immune. If you have blood and adrenaline coursing through your veins, like most of us, you have only one defense against auction fever: *Set a top price on the piece you want, and don't bid beyond it.* That is the Second Commandment of auction buying.

Now you're probably wondering how you're going to set a top price, aren't you? And perhaps you're even wondering what the *First* Commandment of auction buying is. Well, they're interrelated. The First Commandment is this: *Never bid on anything at an auction unless you have examined it before the auction begins.* Virtually every auction house and auctioneer in the country will give you this preview privilege—on the same day as the auction or several days ahead of time—and if you don't take advantage of it, it's the same as bidding with a blindfold on. Examining what interests you at the preview will give you time to set your top price. If you're not yet knowledgeable enough to know what a piece might bring at auction, and what it might be worth, you can always visit a few shops or flea markets and see what they are selling similar pieces for. Furthermore, the preview gives you the opportunity to determine firsthand the structural condition of the items that appeal to you.

Having followed the two commandments of auction buying—and there are only two—you may now consider yourself immune to auction fever.

Types of Auctions. As a used-furniture buyer, you are fortunate, for there are many more types of auctions for you than there are for the buyer of earlier antiques. Auction-house sales, estate sales, sheriff's sales, bankruptcy sales, unclaimed-freight sales at moving and storage companies and even at the U.S. Post Office (the latter generally held annually), restaurant and hotel going-out-of-business sales—those are only a few. Most of them will be advertised in your local newspapers and in the antiques periodicals, and many auctioneers and auction houses will notify you of upcoming sales if you place your name on their mailing lists. Sometimes an auction house will send you an illustrated brochure or catalog for each sale, but there is usually a charge for the latter.

Conditions of Sale. This is an annotated list, usually posted somewhere in an auction house or printed in an auction catalog, that outlines the method and philosophy of a particular auction house. Reading and understanding it will help you to have a better feel for how an auction works and to gain confidence in your bidding. Ignoring the conditions of sale is the same as not reading the "fine print" in an insurance policy.

If the auction you're planning to attend has no catalog and if no conditions of sale seem to be posted anywhere, ask the auctioneer or the clerk at the preview about them. Here is a typical list of the conditions of sale of an auction house, plus some comments.

"1. Warranty: We guarantee the age, condition, and authenticity of each lot [item or group of items] *to be as represented in the catalog, or at the time of sale."* This is a good thing,

since many auction houses make absolutely no warranty, and each lot is sold "as is." Note, however, the phrase "at the time of sale"; this means that anything the auctioneer says about a lot during the sale, which may differ from the catalog description, takes precedence over the catalog description.

"2. Reserve bids: All of our sales are unrestricted. This is a legal term to show that each lot will be sold to the highest bidder regardless of price and that the owner cannot reserve the item or buy it back." In other words, this auction house, unlike some other auction houses, does not permit the consignor of a lot to set a secret reserve price below which the item will not be sold. In auctions where reserves are permitted, and where the highest bid does not reach the reserve, the lot is said to have been "bought back" by the consignor.

"3. Absentee bids: If you wish to leave an absentee bid, it will be given to an experienced bidder in the audience to execute competitively and buy as cheaply as possible." This means that if you cannot attend the auction in person, you may still leave a bid with the house. If you are the high bidder, you may win the lot for *less* than your high bid. For example, if the bidding is going up in ten-dollar "advances," and the high bid from the audience is seventy dollars, any absentee bid for eighty dollars or more will win the lot; even if your absentee bid was two hundred dollars, you'd still get the lot for eighty.

"4. Protested bids: The auctioneer is the sole determiner as to who is the successful bidder." This is self-explanatory.

How to Bid. There are a lot of tricky methods of bidding, other than the straightforward method of hanging in there until you reach your top price. (You hope, of course, that you *won't* reach your top price!) For example, some auction pros start the bidding at a very high price hoping to shock the competition into not bidding at all. However, for first-timers I recommend the simplest bidding method, which is often used by the pros: Just wave your hand in front of your chest, or nod for each bid, and stay

with it until you are the successful bidder or are knocked
out of the auction.

Why am I spending so much time on auctions? Because
in my opinion they are one of the best places to acquire
bargains in used furniture. At almost every auction I've
ever attended, used furniture has sold for less than what
it was going for in the shops. This is largely because the
private buyer has an advantage over the dealers at an
auction: The dealer must buy at a price that allows him
or her to make a later profit; but the private buyer does
not have to figure in any profit markup and therefore can
often outbid the dealers.

Remember that what's important is not whether the
auctioneer is honest, or whether there are a lot of dealers
bidding against you, or whether the competition from
private buyers is fierce. What's important is to buy what
you want at the right price. If the price is too high, don't
buy. And chalk up the auction to experience.

Flea Markets

Like auctions, flea markets are advertised in local newspapers and in the antiques periodicals, and lately more and
more advertisements have been appearing as the number
of markets grows by leaps and bounds. A good flea market—or "flea," as they are often called—can be a great
stalking ground for the used-furniture bargain hunter.
But all flea markets are not created equal, and you should
be aware of the three basic types: permanent fleas, transient fleas, and special fleas.

Permanent Fleas. These are often indoor markets, and
they are really nothing more than a lot of separate little
shops or stalls. They're like a big street with a lot of shops,
and everyone knows what everyone else has to sell and
what it's selling for because the dealers are permanent
stall-holders. As a result there is much less competition
among dealers and more possibilities for "price fixing."
Furthermore, since indoor, permanent fleas usually open
to the dealers before they open to the public, the dealers
get first crack at each other's merchandise—in the trade,
the merchandise is said to have been "picked over." Each

Figure 2

A rainstorm never discourages the
true bargain hunter from going to
a flea market.

time a dealer buys from another dealer and sells to still another dealer, the price of the merchandise goes up because of the profit markup. By the time *you* buy the piece, the price might be far higher than it was when the flea market opened, but, of course, you didn't have a chance at it at the lowest price. You may find a bargain at a permanent flea, it's true, but on the whole a permanent flea is not nearly as interesting to the bargain hunter as a transient flea.

Transient Fleas. These are usually outdoor markets and they occasionally adjoin permanent, indoor flea markets. They almost always open very early in the morning—at sunup or before, in fact—and if you don't get there when it begins to get light out, you'll be fated to stay in the dark about the bargain opportunities at transient fleas. For at a transient flea everyone has the same chance for a bargain as everyone else because the market opens at the same time to dealers and bargain hunters alike. If you want bargains, you'll have to *join* the bargain hunters; believe me, there's no way to fight them.

Special Fleas. These are simply transient fleas that are heavily advertised. The first special fleas of each year are usually the grand opening for the season of each outdoor flea market—the season generally running from mid-April to mid-October. All winter long the dealers have been building their inventory, just waiting for the opportunity to sell their wares at the first special fleas of the season. For that reason the special fleas may attract two or three times the normal complement of selling dealers. Once the season is in full swing, the managements of the various markets may dream up other reasons for holding special fleas—a long holiday weekend is as good an excuse as any—and so the entire flea-market season may be punctuated with heavily advertised special fleas. As you can imagine, they are often a bargain hunter's paradise because of the sheer number of dealers and the quantity of merchandise.

Antiques Shows

More and more the items that are turning up at antiques shows are not antiques at all but used merchandise and "collectibles"—those items that are too old to be simply called used, and too new to be called antiques. Thus antiques shows can be a good place to buy used furniture, especially pieces made between about 1870 and 1915. In addition, shows make it fairly easy for you to compare the prices asked by many different dealers and to get an idea of what the dealers think is selling well in the current market. (After all, they can't drag everything in their inventories to a show, and so they must be selective about what they do bring.) Unfortunately, antiques shows can suffer from the same problem that permanent flea markets have, namely, picked-over merchandise: The doors don't open to the public until a specified time, and by then many good pieces may have changed hands. At the fine antiques shows, that sort of thing is outlawed by the management; but the fine shows usually have only very old, and very expensive, pieces.

You can find out about shows from the newspapers, antiques periodicals, and roadside signs. Furthermore, many dealers will have printed cards in their shops that not only advertise the shows but that will also be worth a discount on the admission fees.

Antiques Shops

Many of the same dealers who do the show circuit also have shops, and many antiques shops are little more than used-furniture stores, so of course you'll be able to find what you're looking for in some of them. But even in the shops that really do sell antiques you may be able to find a bargain or two. For example, a shop that specializes in above-average Victorian furniture may have a few pieces of Golden Oak or Mission furniture on hand. Since the dealer does not specialize in Golden Oak, he or she may want to get rid of it cheaply. This situation arises because dealers are sometimes forced to buy an entire household of furniture in order to get a few things they really want; they then have to "wholesale" what they consider the "runts" of their latest litter in order not to tie up their capital. But what is a runt to a dealer may be a thoroughbred to you. I've found many bargains in shops that do not specialize in what I'm after.

Like dandelions in spring, these shops are sprouting up everywhere. A suburban community that may have had one such shop several years ago may now have three or four right on Main Street. And many of these shops are now occupying urban downtown storefronts of businesses that have moved to the suburbs. Basically there are two kinds of secondhand shops: "junkies" and "jazzies." Here's a brief rundown on both.

Secondhand Shops

Junkies. These shops sell what could euphemistically be called "unselected goods." In other words, they're volume operations that buy in bulk lots of household goods ranging from sewing machines to sinks to sofas. Since the entire lot was purchased for one price, the management may not be overly concerned with the niceties of various pieces of used furniture, and resale prices will reflect this. A bargain-minded picker can find good buys.

Jazzies. These shops are more choosy about what they sell. They may specialize in certain items and may have catchy names like "The Second Time Around" or "Granny's Attic." They may even use the word *antique* in their names.

Selectivity may of course mean higher prices, but there are advantages to patronizing these shops. For one thing, you may be able to leave a deposit on an item and then get it back if you change your mind. For another, you won't have to machete your way through a jungle of miscellaneous unselected goods. But you should remember one rule about the jazzier shops: "Never before Christmas, and not in the country during the summer." Prices are always inflated just before Christmas, and during the summer prices in vacation spots and in well-traveled antiques areas are higher than they would be in the off-season.

For those reasons you should do your shopping after Labor Day, when many shops try to clear out as much inventory as possible prior to closing for the winter. The best time to buy in the country is in the early spring, when the shops are well stocked in anticipation of summer business, but cash is short. Besides, it's the time when Uncle Sam dips into everyone's pocket, and the hoped-for seasonal customers are still a couple of months away.

Consignment, Resale, and Thrift Shops

A few decades ago these shops—which sell items on behalf of private owners for a commission of about twenty to thirty percent—were operated principally for the benefit of charitable, philanthropic, and religious organizations. Now, as another reflection of the used boom, a large contingent of strictly commercial shops (meaning that the management keeps the commissions) has joined the original group of consignment sellers. The proprietors are often middle-aged suburbanites whose family responsibilities have tapered off, and they tend to set prices realistically and reasonably. Some consignment shops focus on specific periods or types of merchandise, and many of them have a policy of end-of-the-month markdowns on the prices of items that haven't sold.

Stripping and Refinishing Shops

Some of these shops sell used furniture, using slack periods to refinish and repair the pieces they have for sale. Occasionally they have unclaimed items that they're happy to move out for the cost of the labor they've put into them.

Amateur Sales

Garage, yard, barn, tag, porch, and lawn sales—all of these are usually conducted by a family or group of families that are moving or for some other reason consolidating their belongings for one reason or another (to pay the bills?). From the bargain hunter's point of view, the genuinely interesting sales are those that last for only a day or two—usually one weekend—as opposed to those that boil down to a permanent "Porch Sale" sign in the yard and an immutable collection of family junk under the eaves. The bulk of these home-style sales are held during the prime moving and cleaning seasons—spring through fall. Announcements of the sale may appear in the local paper or may simply take the form of handmade signs nailed to a utility pole.

The age and selection of furniture at amateur sales are wildly unpredictable. Surprises abound, both good and bad. As for pricing, it's likely to be erratic. Most people have an inflated idea of what their property is worth. Setting prices realistically takes solid experience, and those without it are likely both to over- and underprice in seemingly random ways.

When you decide whether or not to attend an amateur sale, don't let the neighborhood deceive you. I've seen abominable, undistinguished stuff—literally on its last legs—fought over on the verdant front lawns of new, prestigious suburban communities; I've also seen good used furniture go begging in older, lower-income neighborhoods. In the latter, by the way, the probabilities are far higher that the furniture will be in the lifetime-purchase category and that it will have been well maintained. In the wealthier neighborhoods the purchasing of disposable items is far more rampant, and pieces that will be changed frequently to suit decorating whims are often as shabby as the motives for buying them in the first place.

Estate and Household Liquidation Sales

When all or a substantial portion of the furnishings of a home are offered for sale on the premises, the owners usually hire a professional sales agent to orchestrate the proceedings. These agents are generally experts at their business, especially at pricing things realistically. In many cases a preview is scheduled when you can look over the merchandise. The sale itself may last for two or three days in an "everything-must-go" atmosphere, with prices on sold items marked down on the last day. Occasionally a sale may combine the effects of more than one household, which adds variety and interest.

Bazaars, Fairs, and Rummage Sales

Church, school, and auxiliary organizations sponsor these day-long affairs, and the "good cause" is likely to flush out hidden treasures from the donors' attics and basements. You can expect good values, too, because the people who run these events usually have years of experience in pricing to sell.

When a building, such as a hotel or a theater, is being demolished, the contents must be sold pronto. The wrecking company itself may conduct the sale, or it may hire an agent. In either case such sales are a superb source not only of used furniture but also of architectural decorations, doors, fireplace mantels, plumbing hardware, and more. These sales are usually advertised in the newspaper and sometimes on radio or television as well. Get there early for the best buys.

Wrecking Companies

Moving companies often hold an annual sale or auction of unclaimed merchandise. Such sales can be a gold mine for the bargain prospector. I've seen used furniture, especially from the thirties and later, sell for only a fraction of its market value. The only trouble with these sales is that there always seems to be an endless number of unopened cartons of plastic dishes, rusty gardening tools, and ten-year-old clothing that must be sold before the furniture goes on the block. But if you're in the market for that sort of thing too, a day spent at a warehouse sale can be very profitable.

Moving and Storage Companies

I have personally sold used furniture through the classifieds, and at what now seem like bargain prices, so I know the classifieds can be a good and plentiful source of used-furniture bargains. Some advertisements that seem authentic may have been placed by dealers, so you'd do well to ask the person who says hello if he is a private party or a dealer before getting too enthusiastic about an ad. On the other hand, most of the ads are placed by private parties who simply want to get rid of two or three items that have been taking up room in the attic, or by amateur fixer-uppers who are trying to make a little money on the side. Check out the classifieds under the "Household Goods," "For the Home," and "Furniture" categories.

Classified Advertisements

Garbage Dumps and Street Corners

Don't stick up your nose at garbage dumps, especially those in the country. You'd be amazed at the perfectly usable things that are burned, buried, or simply abandoned every day, and that includes furniture. Of course, those without the stomach for thrashing through trash would be well advised to catch used furniture before the garbage people pick it up, and that means casing the highways and byways on garbage-pickup day. Some of my friends have become superscavengers and have found Golden Oak furniture that would make many a dealer's heart jump for joy. And the "price" was right, to say the least.

The Artful Bargainer

Unquestionably the most logical place to look for used furniture is a used-furniture shop. Some shops may specialize in certain periods or even certain types of merchandise—brass beds is a currently popular category. Others may sell anything the proprietor can acquire at a price that leaves some room for profit. But whatever the shop sells, the question inevitably arises in the bargain hunter's mind: "Is the price marked on a piece the lowest price? Is it the best the dealer will do?"

If you are already an artful bargainer, you're familiar with the techniques of making the best deal possible when there's room for negotiation. If you're not, here are a few suggestions.

Be Congenial. This may sound slightly inane, but I think it's good to remember that proprietors and sales people have feelings. Many of them are quite sensitive about the quality of what they sell, and nothing will turn them against you faster—and make them less willing to bargain —than taciturnly poking through their shops with a look on your face as though someone had just passed a dead fish under your nose. But being congenial—saying hello to the shopkeeper, perhaps praising a piece or two—is the first step in demonstrating that you are a customer worthy of a bargain. It makes the shopkeeper feel that he or she is more than just another piece of used furniture.

Check the Price Tags. Ask yourself if the prices are in line with—or above or below—other prices you have noted in other shops, flea markets, and the like. Keep in mind that many dealers have a two- or even three-tier pricing system: the price marked on the tag, a somewhat lower price, and a rock-bottom price. Sometimes a discount price will even be marked on the tag in code. For example, a tag may have a price of $175, but in another spot on the same tag may be the small notation "D150." That means that the shop owner is willing to sell the piece to another dealer ("D") for $150. You may be able to get the piece for that price, too, or somewhere in between $150 and $175. Or perhaps the tag says something like "D051"; that's the same discount code, except backward. One dealer I know has an even trickier code. On the same $175 piece, his coded price might read "D2300." It's the same discount price; to find it, divide 300 by 2.

Find a Flaw or Two. Since you've established yourself as a nice, congenial person—which, of course, you really are—you now have earned the "privilege" of faultfinding. Virtually no piece of used furniture is in perfect condition, and a flaw may be a wedge you can drive in to lower the price of a piece. Does the piece have a veneered top, while others in the same style have solid-wood tops? Is the piece stained a little, or dented? Does it need a few repairs that are not particularly easy to make? All of those and more might be price-lowering flaws. The idea is not to, as they say in the trade, "knock" the piece, but to subtly point out that something is ever so slightly wrong.

Be Humble but Firm. Make it clear any way you can that you admire the piece and wish you could pay the marked price (humble), but that you will have no qualms about letting it go if you can't get a lower price (firm). That doesn't mean you should threaten the dealer—"If you don't give me a price break I'll walk out of here and never come back!" or "The shop down the street has the same piece for twenty-five dollars less, so why don't you?" It means, rather, that you should ask, or possibly even assume, that a lower price can be had. Say, for example, "The price is a little high for me, but I can give you such-and-such for it." The dealer may not meet your offer, but he or she may make a counteroffer that is lower than the marked price.

By the way, here's the phrase the pros often use: "How much do you *need* to get for that piece?" I use that one all the time. It's experienced-bargainer talk.

Get a Discount on a Volume Purchase. A dealer may not be willing or able to go lower on a single piece—say, a table—but throw in a chair and a lamp and he or she may have more margin to work with. Perhaps you'll pay the marked price on the table and get something off on the other items, or perhaps everything will get marked down. Either way, you've struck a bargain, and the dealer's profit margin hasn't suffered. Remember that the point of all bargaining is to seek a fair and common ground that allows the dealer a profit and you a good buy.

Swap. Suppose you've got a piece of used furniture at home that, for one reason or another, you'd like to get rid of. Suppose further that it seems to be the sort of piece the dealer could sell. A good move might be to propose a swap: your piece at home for the one in the shop. I've made great bargains this way, especially when I hadn't paid much for my swap piece.

Pay in Installments. Many a dealer is quite willing to let you pay for a piece in installments with no interest or storage charges as long as you allow the dealer to hold the piece as collateral until it's paid for. Although it's not strictly speaking a bargaining method, if you're strapped for cash it can be an excellent way to get the piece of furniture you want and still have enough money in the bank to feed and clothe yourself. If you take this installment approach, be sure to get the terms of the deal on paper, making certain that there will be no interest or storage fees.

Here are a few final words of wisdom. The suggestions have been gleaned from many years of experience in buying, and sometimes reselling, in the used and the antiques marketplace. Ignore them at your peril!

The Voice of Experience

Get a Descriptive Receipt. Although none of us would ever think of buying a camera or a washing machine without getting a receipt, many receiptless transactions take place in the used marketplace. Indeed, a few dealers never give receipts unless they're asked by the customer, and then the receipts they do give might not be adequate.

What is an adequate receipt? It's one that describes the piece, giving such details as its age, the wood or woods it's made of, and perhaps any restorations that have been done to it. A receipt, you see, is actually a contract between buyer and seller, in which the seller, in effect, guarantees the piece to be what he or she says it is and the buyer agrees to pay a certain price for it. Now, suppose you discover that the piece is not made of the wood the dealer said it was, or the piece is of the wrong period, or the piece disintegrates after your cat rubs against it. Without a proper, descriptive receipt, you'd be stuck; with a receipt, you can return the piece. If the piece is really defective in some way, and the dealer refuses to take it back, you then have legal recourse.

And one more thing: An adequate receipt is also one that has the dealer's or the shop's name and address on it, either stamped, printed, or written in the dealer's hand. An anonymous receipt is worth about as much as was a ticket for the maiden voyage of the *Titanic.*

Get a Tax Resale Number, If You Wish. A tax resale number is issued to you by your state tax office or other state office. It allows you to buy merchandise—used furniture, for example—without paying sales tax, if you intend to resell the merchandise sometime in the future. In effect, having a tax number makes you a dealer, and eligible for any discounts available to dealers from other dealers.

Sounds great, doesn't it? Since almost everyone eventually resells something he has purchased, why doesn't everyone have a tax number? One of the best reasons is that along with the tax number come responsibilities. For one thing, you'll have to file a quarterly statement with your state tax office listing all your purchases and sales. For another, some state tax offices will not accept out-of-state tax numbers; for example, Massachusetts requires dealers to use a Massachusetts tax number in that state, regardless of where the dealer resides.

If you're interested in getting your own tax number, I suggest you talk it over with an accountant, who will explain the ramifications in greater detail.

Buy across State Lines. Many people are not aware of the fact that if they buy something in one state and have it delivered to another, they pay no state sales tax. Most mail-order buyers know this, but they tend to forget it when they purchase other point-of-sale items. Since I live on the border of another state, I try to buy in that state and have things delivered in my state. I've saved a bit of money this way, and perhaps you can, too.

Buy Resalable Items. Perhaps you think that whatever piece of used furniture you buy today, you'll have ten years from now. But in practice things don't usually work out that way. You may tire of the piece, or you may upgrade your furniture collection (that is, buy better, usually more expensive items), or you may simply need to raise some cash in a hurry. For these reasons it's not in your best interests to buy pieces that are so outrageous, or shoddy, or quirky, that no one else will ever want them. If possible try to buy pieces that not only please your own tastes but that will be desirable to others when the time comes to resell.

Buy the Best You Can Afford. Your impulse, especially if you have a large area to furnish, may be to buy as many pieces as you can, as quickly and as cheaply as possible, with the idea that later you can sell off and replace what no longer appeals to you. But I have found that in the long run one reaps psychological as well as financial rewards from buying the best used furniture possible, even if that means buying a piece here and a piece there over a period of time.

The psychological rewards come from being secure in the knowledge that each piece you own is of high quality. A growing contempt for cheap goods is only natural, and you certainly don't want to surround yourself with items you come to despise as you become more and more sophisticated about what is and is not the best. Buying the best pays off financially, too, because almost inevitably the best increases in value faster than the mediocre, not to mention the shoddy. Put another way, a relatively expensive, high-quality piece can be a better bargain than a mediocre piece at half the price.

Quality, both in construction and design, is discussed throughout this book, and I hope that my insights on the subject will help you develop your own ideas about why one piece is better than another.

Buy "In the Rough." When a piece is in the rough, it means that it needs some restoration, or repairs, or both. It also means a lower price, since the cost of any work done to a piece must necessarily be added to its selling price. Thus if you are at all handy, or if you want to learn how to be handy—which I will cover in Chapter 5—it behooves you, the bargain hunter, to buy pieces in the rough when possible, and fix them up yourself.

You should also be aware of the fact that what some dealers call "in the rough" should instead be called "untouched condition." That may sound like a euphemism, but it isn't, for some pieces need no repairs or serious restoration at all but simply need their finishes revived a little. To some dealers that makes no difference; they just cannot get it out of their heads that any piece with an old finish must be stripped and refinished, which adds to the cost of the piece, of course. Some buyers think that way as well. But believe me, that's a mistake. I can almost guarantee you that some day, not too far in the future, pieces with their original finishes will sell for far more than those that have been refinished. This is already occurring in certain collecting areas—with Mission furniture, for example—and in my opinion the trend is bound to continue and expand.

The same refinishing mania we are witnessing today in the used-furniture market struck the early American antiques market in the 1920s. Thousand of great pieces had their original, mellow finishes removed to make them nice and shiny and new looking. Today most of those refinished pieces are worth only a fraction of those that have their original finishes still intact.

If you must have your furniture brand-new and shiny looking, feel free to disagree with me. But consider yourself warned.

2

---❦---

THE MAIN INGREDIENT: WOOD

WHY WOOD? Why is the main ingredient in most period furniture—in most furniture, period—wood?

Perhaps the reasons are obvious, but I think I should enumerate them anyway: Wood can be riven, sawed, carved, turned, joined, bent, and shaped more easily than virtually any other material. And as if that weren't enough, it's also strong for its weight. Consider, for example, not only the difficulty in making a suite of living-room furniture out of rock, but the difficulty in trying to move it to vacuum under it. Or consider the fact that hickory has a greater tensile strength than steel.

For centuries wood has shaped the evolution and individual lives of human beings—in fuels, tools, weapons, buildings, wheels, boats, eating utensils, paper, and more, as well as in furniture. And we have returned the compliment, endlessly shaping wood to our needs. Today furniture may be made of materials other than wood, it's true. But good wood has never lost its status as the hallmark of quality in furniture.

Thus, for the buyer of furniture—used or otherwise—a knowledge of the kinds and characteristics of wood seems to me indispensable.

Hardwoods and Softwoods

Lumber is usually divided into two large categories: hardwoods and softwoods. Hardwoods come from flowering trees with broad leaves that generally fall off in the autumn; for example, maple, oak, walnut, cherry, birch, and poplar. Softwoods come from cone-bearing trees that don't usually lose their leaves (needles), at least not all at once; for example, pine, redwood, larch, spruce, hemlock, and cedar.

The terms *hardwood* and *softwood* do not refer to the actual hardness or softness of the woods. To use an extreme example, southern shortleaf pine, technically a softwood, is considerably harder than balsa, a hardwood. You can see, therefore, that a label describing a piece of furniture as made from "Selected Hardwoods" does not necessarily mean that the furniture is of high quality or inherently durable. Good furniture is furniture that is made of *hard woods* but not always of *hardwoods.* Please keep the distinction in mind.

Trees that produce hard woods grow far more slowly than those that produce soft woods. As a result, hard woods tend to be densely grained and tough, all muscle and fiber and no fat. This quality alone would make hard woods desirable for furniture that must withstand stress and wear, but it is only one of the reasons for using them. Hard woods can also be turned and carved more cleanly and with more sharply defined edges than soft woods. Furthermore, hard woods can usually be sanded and finished very smoothly. Add to these practical reasons the fact that many hard woods have a beautiful grain or color and you'll understand why hard woods are used in fine furniture.

Unfortunately, like many things of superior quality, hard woods have never been as plentiful as woods that are soft. The trees that produce hard woods simply do not replenish themselves as quickly as those that produce soft woods, and besides, with the exception of some tropical hardwoods, the trees don't yield as many usable furniture boards. Since they are in shorter supply, hard woods have always been more expensive than soft woods. That is particularly true of the most beautiful hard woods, some of which, like black walnut, have been exploited to the point of becoming endangered species.

Since it would be wasteful not to lavish good craftsmanship on furniture made with expensive, rare ingredients, almost all furniture made of hard woods is well constructed; and the more beautiful the wood, the better the craftsmanship. For example, a Golden Oak piece that is really made of solid oak will usually be better than one for which chestnut or elm was substituted. That's also true of many pieces in which solid hard woods and veneers have been combined, especially if they were made prior to the 1920s or after about 1945. (Furniture made during the interim presents unique problems, which are discussed in Chapter 10.)

Obviously, then, it's to your advantage to train yourself to distinguish one species of wood from another. Verbal descriptions won't help much, but color swatches or actual wood samples will give you a good start. In the "Further Reading" section of this book I've listed some publications that incorporate these visual aids. There are other clues you can look for, as well, and perhaps labels are the best.

A piece that is labeled, tagged, or stenciled with the word *genuine* preceding the name of the wood—"Genuine Walnut" or "Genuine Mahogany," for example—will have all its exposed parts made of that wood. On the other hand, any other description will be a "weasel-word" way of obfuscating the material that's been used, usually by describing the color and not the wood itself. "Early American Walnut," "Imperial Oak," and "Regency Mahogany" are species of trees that root only in the minds of advertising copywriters.

Four Surface Characteristics of Lumber

Grain, figure, luster, and color—those four characteristics, taken together, will determine the quality and desirability of furniture woods. Thus they are points to look for when assessing a piece of furniture that has large exposed areas of wood.

Grain. This refers to the direction or arrangement of the fibrous wood cells, especially the annual growth rings. The appearance of the grain on the surface of a board is often determined by the way the board has been sawed

Figure 4

Top: The grain pattern in this plain-sawed oak board is a series of *V*'s. *Bottom:* This quarter-sawed mahogany board has a straight grain with an interesting figure.

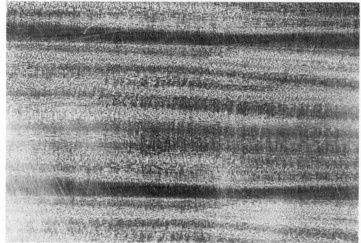

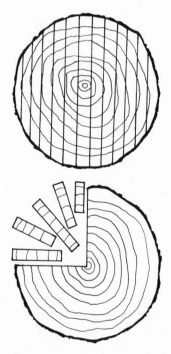

Figure 3

Top: In plain-sawing, as many boards as possible are sawed from the log with parallel cuts. *Bottom:* In quarter-sawing, the log is quartered before the boards are cut from it. The quarter-sawed log yields fewer boards than the plain-sawed one.

from the log. For example, plain- or flat-sawing produces a series of V's or ellipses, while quarter-sawing produces a relatively straight grain (figures 3 and 4).

Figure. This is a natural pattern in a board, in addition to the normal grain, produced by grain deviations, rays, knots, and the like. Quarter-sawing tends to bring out the figure in a board. The bird's-eye and curly figures (the latter also called tiger or fiddle-back) are perhaps the most common (see figure 76). Note that a board may have a distinctive grain but no figure at all; conversely, it may have an interesting figure but an inconspicuous grain.

Luster. Lumber with a natural luster seems to have an inner, three-dimensional, satinlike glow. Indeed, West Indian satinwood is named after its remarkable luster. The "glow" is caused by the cell walls reflecting light at various angles, similar to the effect of reflective tape for automobiles. Quarter-sawing emphasizes the luster in lumber, and the luster itself will emphasize any natural figure in the wood.

Color. The natural color of lumber is a factor in its desirability as a furniture wood. Walnut and mahogany have excellent color; poplar has an undesirable greenish hue; birch is simply bland and uninteresting. Of course, the natural color of lumber is often intensified or changed artificially—for instance, by staining, steaming, bleaching, or fuming with ammonia gas.

Now, the foregoing is not to suggest that every piece of used wooden furniture must exhibit the finest of all five surface characteristics. If that were so, I'd buy nothing but fiddle-back mahogany furniture, which would be about as interesting as listening to the same record over and over. On the other hand, I do like furniture with lots of wood showing, and I like that furniture to be as appealing as possible, given the limitations of the particular wood it's made from. If you feel the same way, then an awareness of the surface characteristics of lumber should help you to recognize one aspect of quality in used furniture.

Solid Woods

The very words have a ring of quality about them, promising something durable and valuable. Frequently the promise is fulfilled. But solid wood alone is not a guarantee of quality, for several reasons.

A Moving Experience. Look at a piece of solid-wood furniture. It's just sitting there, not doing anything in particular, right?

Wrong. The wood is moving, not enough to clock it on a radar screen, but moving nonetheless. No matter how old it is, or how well seasoned, solid wood will shrink and expand depending on the environment's temperature and humidity. And shrinkage and expansion lead to warping, twisting, and cracking of solid boards. Most used furniture has been around for a long enough time so that if it was going to warp, twist, or crack, it probably already has. Nevertheless, removing a solid-wood piece from a damp barn or shop to a dry, centrally heated home can start the process all over again. It's something to keep in mind when buying solid-wood furniture. Also, be aware that quarter-sawed boards are far less susceptible to the effects of shrinkage and expansion than are plain-sawed boards.

Strong, dark, and boring. Solid-wood furniture may be relatively strong and nicely finished, but it also may be boring. Why? Because almost all solid-wood furniture is made from hardwoods that are in plentiful supply, and they are plentiful because they lack an interesting grain, have an objectionable natural color, or for other reasons. Red oak, for example, has large pores and a raw, pinkish hue that is difficult to disguise. And maple has the opposite problem: it's almost the ideal furniture wood except for its bland, undistinguished grain.

The point of all this is that you should not be swayed simply because a piece happens to be made from solid wood.

Veneer

In the minds of many people, *veneer* connotes sham and pretense. Obviously, they feel, those thin top layers of veneer have been used to cover up some undesirable wood underneath. But that is not always the case, for the purpose of veneer is usually to create a surface that is more beautiful, varied, and exotic than a solid-wood surface ever could be.

Veneering is an old practice, going back several centuries. Back then, a piece of sawed veneer might be as thick as 1/8 inch. Today, veneer on fine furniture varies between 1/20 and 1/30 inch; if necessary, veneer can be cut down to 1/100 inch.

The years 1900 to 1920 took veneering from a simply decorative process to an industrialized one as well—a means of turning out inexpensive, mass-produced furni-

Indiana Lumber and Veneer Co.

INDIANAPOLIS, IND.

Manufacturers of

Sawed and Sliced Veneers and Band Sawed Lumber.

Specially Veneer Sawed Quartered Oak.
We Carry Complete Stocks at our Warerooms.

L. P. HOLLOWELL, Agent.
New York Furniture Exchange, New York City.

CHAS. McQUEWAN, Agent.
89 Campau St., Grand Rapids, Mich.

Varieties of figure peculiar to Quartered Sawed Oak Veneer as manufactured by the Indiana Lumber and Veneer Co., Indianapolis, Indiana.

ture. The new machines could slice veneers thinner than before, and they could trim and paste the edges together to form large sheets. Most important, huge, lathelike peeling machines could strip veneers from logs in continuous sheets instead of slicing them.

But veneering should not always be abhorred. It makes rare woods less expensive to use, and veneers can be matched and seamed together to create lovely symmetrical patterns. Plain-sawed veneers will have a Gothic-archlike appearance, which is appropriately called a cathedral pattern. Quarter-sawing will create a straight, or comb, pattern. In oak veneer, quarter-sawing produces elongated "flashes"—the hallmark of the best oak furniture (figures 5 and 20).

The practice of veneering also allows furniture manufacturers to utilize wood from sections of a tree that have a particularly pronounced and beautiful natural grain pattern. If not sliced into veneers, those sections might yield only a few solid pieces or might have to be discarded altogether. The crotch—the point where the branches fan out from the trunk—is one of those sections. Crotch veneers evoke the feeling of the muscles and sinews of the tree. The section of the log closest to the root will yield a flamelike pattern. Veneer cut from burls—tumorlike excrescences on trees—have textured patterns with intricate whorls.

Finally, veneers cut from different species of trees can be combined in a single piece of furniture to create even more intricate designs. Much used furniture is veneered, and I'll have more to say about it in Chapter 5.

Plywood

Earlier in this chapter I mentioned that solid wood can warp, twist, and crack from shrinkage and expansion. First patented in 1865 in the form we know it today, plywood virtually eliminates those problems.

Plywood is an assembly of layers (plies) of thick veneer in combination with a lumber core, joined with an adhesive. Each ply is arranged with its grain running at right angles to the ply immediately adjoining it (crossbanding). The result: the effect of shrinkage in one layer is counteracted by shrinkage in the layer adjoining it, and the entire assembly remains straight.

Plywood can be made as thin as 1/10 inch and as thick as necessary. And as you may have guessed, thin plywood is more susceptible to changes in humidity and temperature than is the thicker stuff. When made from hardwoods, the plies will usually have been peeled from the fast-growing, fairly common varieties—poplar, gum, willow, bass, and all the trees that grow to a good size but do not have a particularly beautiful grain.

Plywood, of course, can itself be veneered. It can also be produced in uniform sizes (today's is generally four by eight feet). The use of plywood in furniture does not necessarily imply low quality.

The Perfect Core

By the 1950s a completely new type of core had come on the scene, ultimately replacing all the others in straight-sided furniture. It's made from chips, flakes, or particles of wood that are dried, mixed with resin glues, and then pressed between huge hot platens. This stuff has various trade names, but is generally called particle- , chip- , or flakeboard, depending on whether it is made from saw-dust-size particles or cornflake-size shavings.

Flakeboard cores are so smooth and stable that they don't require crossbanding, like conventional plywood. The stuff is almost impossible to dent. And because virtually any kind of wood and all parts of a tree save the bark can be used in manufacturing it, it's relatively inexpensive. Originally it was used only in inexpensive furniture. Recently, however, quality manufacturers in this country and abroad have been using it extensively; it is the only core used on expensive European furniture.

All in all, it's an excellent product. The only problem with flakeboard, if it can be called a problem, is that furniture made from it is Heavy, with a capital H.

Well, now you know more than ninety-nine percent of all furniture buyers about the main ingredient in what they are buying. Now it's time to move on to another quality factor in furniture: construction.

3

CASING THE JOINTS:
FURNITURE CONSTRUCTION

ALTHOUGH ONE PROBABLY EXISTS somewhere, I can't remember ever seeing a piece of furniture that was carved from a single, solid block of wood. Instead, wooden furniture is composed of many different structural and nonstructural parts that, one way or another, are connected to each other. Obviously a piece of furniture that is well connected will last longer than one that isn't. And an ability to recognize the difference is important because it can protect you from plunking down your money for an apparent precious gem of a piece that turns out to be nothing but cheap glass.

As you read through this chapter, please keep in mind that I am not urging you to buy only furniture of the finest construction. What I'm really getting at is that, in choosing between two pieces of similar design and price, the better made will be the better buy.

Joints

The point at which two furniture parts come together is a joint. Indeed, certain early furniture makers were called "joyners" because they specialized in attaching furniture parts together.

Some joints are inherently strong and others weak. The best joints are those that provide the most contact area between wood and wood, or those that, when glued, provide an extra measure of gluing surface. But the use of a particular joint at a particular point on a piece of furniture is dictated not only by practical considerations but also by esthetic ones: If you tailor the joint to the design, you may remove too much wood, and the parts may break at the

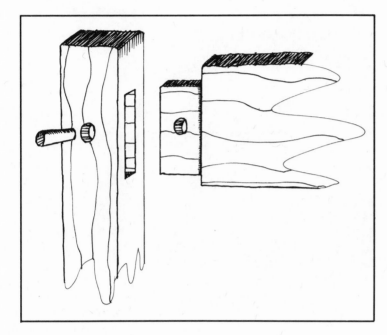

Figure 6

A mortise-and-tenon joint before assembly. The mortise is on the left, the tenon on the right. The peg will be driven through the holes in both parts to lock the joint.

junction of the joint; conversely, if you tailor the design to the joint, the parts may look swollen and grotesque.

The following are a few furniture joints that are worth knowing about.

Mortise-and-Tenon Joint. A mortise is a rectangular hole cut partway or all the way through a piece of wood; a tenon is a rectangular, tonguelike projection cut at the end of another piece of wood. Put the tenon into the mortise, and you've got a mortise-and-tenon joint (figure 6). In addition, drill a hole through both the mortise and the tenon, hammer a wooden peg through the hole, and you've "locked" the joint without using any glue, screws, or nails.

The mortise-and-tenon joint is unquestionably the most durable method of attaching certain furniture parts together. If done correctly, it's almost unbreakable. Unfortunately, you will find few pieces of used furniture

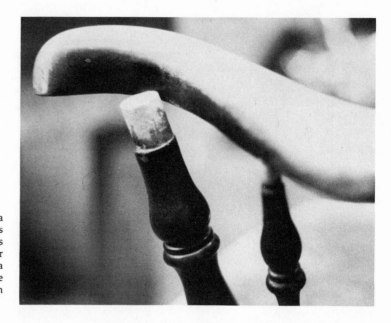

Figure 7

This dowel joint connecting a chair arm to the arm support has come apart because the glue has deteriorated. In this particular joint the dowel is simply a smaller-in-diameter section of the end of the arm support and is an integral part of it.

with true, pegged-together mortise-and-tenon joints because the joint is difficult to make properly without some hand-fitting. One exception to this is Mission furniture made by Gustav Stickley and others (see Chapter 7).

You are likely to find mortise-and-tenon joints where rectangular parts of furniture come together: for example, in chair rungs and legs, legs and seat frames, and arms and arm supports, and in table legs and aprons, and legs and stretchers.

Dowel Joint. In a sense, this is a round version of a mortise-and-tenon joint (figures 7 and 14). The differences are, first, that the dowel is often not an integral part of either piece being joined but is glued into a hole drilled in both pieces; second, the dowel is never pegged; and third, there is much less wood-to-wood contact. A dowel joint can pull or twist apart, and frequently does.

Dowel joints can be found almost anywhere that round-to-round, flat-to-flat, or round-to-flat surfaces are connected.

Dovetail Joint. This is a series of triangular cutouts that fit into another series of triangular cutouts, much like a

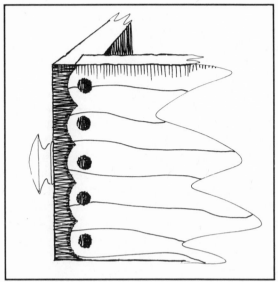

Figure 8 A peg-and-scallop joint on the side of a drawer.

jigsaw puzzle (figure 9). The dovetail has a reputation that almost everyone seems to be familiar with, and the reputation is justified. The joint practically intertwines two pieces of wood, increasing surface contact by about one hundred percent. The joint can neither be pulled backward nor be easily dislodged by lateral pressure, and it holds together all on its own, for the dovetail does not depend on glue for its strength.

Best suited for furniture parts that are square to each other, it is most often found on the sides of drawers. Remember, though, that machine dovetailing is not difficult to do, and wily manufacturers, aware of the dovetail's reputation, have been known to install dovetailed drawers in a piece that otherwise was nothing to write home about.

Peg-and-Scallop Joint. This is a somewhat strange, but not uncommon, form of machine dovetailing that is found on drawers in furniture made from the fourth quarter of the nineteenth century up to about 1915 (figure 8). The peg-and-scallop seems to be an overly complex method of accomplishing a rather simple task, which perhaps explains why it was in vogue for so short a time.

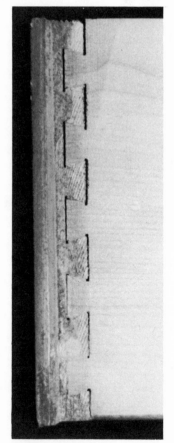

Figure 9

Machine dovetailing on the side of a drawer. Note that although the joint has opened somewhat due to wood shrinkage, the drawer shows no evidence of falling apart.

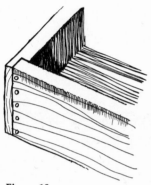

Figure 10

The corner of a rabbet-joined drawer. In this case, the side of the drawer has simply been nailed into its front—not the best method of drawer construction.

Rabbet Joint. A rabbet is a slot or an L-shaped cutout in a furniture part into which another part fits, forming a rabbet joint (figure 10).

The sides of drawers are often rabbeted into the fronts and backs of drawers; it's cheaper and easier to do than a dovetail or a peg-and-scallop, but it's weaker. On the other hand, rabbeting a drawer bottom into the drawer sides is an ideal construction method, far better than simply nailing the bottom in place or using an extra strip of wood to hold it. This is so because the drawer bottom is not held rigidly in place and so can shrink and expand relatively freely, which minimizes cracking. The same comments apply to case pieces—boxlike pieces such as chests of drawers, desks, and cupboards—with paneled sides that are rabbeted in place.

Tongue-and-Groove, Spline, Lap, and Butt Joints. All of these joints are used to create large, flat surfaces from several boards connected together—say, in a table top or chair seat (figure 11). They all work pretty well except for the butt joint, and I'll tell you why.

As I mentioned before, when a board shrinks, it tends to warp or cup. To expand on this point a bit, a board shrinks across its grain, and it "yearns" to warp or cup in a direction opposite to that of its growth rings, as viewed from the end of the board (figure 12). For that reason, boards in a tabletop will be arranged so that their "yearnings" alternate—up, down, up, down, and so on—which counteracts some of the effects of warping.

Boards that have simply been butt-joined together— flat side to flat side—will have a great tendency to pull apart as they shrink and as cracks widen between the boards, regardless of which direction their yearnings face. If boards have been butt-joined in a chair seat or chest top, you'll probably find many of the joints separating— an indication that with stripping or after a dry heating season in your home, the entire top or seat may be like so many pieces of kindling wood (figure 13).

Any of the other methods are superior to butt-joining since the boards are, in effect, locked together, each helping to restrain movement in its neighbor and to minimize warping.

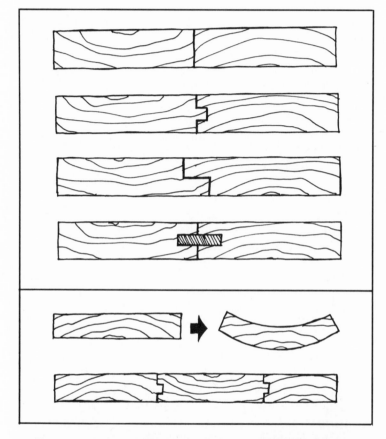

Figure 11

Top to bottom: butt joint; tongue-and-groove joint; lap joint; spline joint.

Figure 12

Top: A board shrinks across its grain and also "yearns" to warp in a direction opposite to that of its growth rings. *Bottom:* By alternating the direction of the yearnings in adjacent boards, warpage is minimized.

Figure 13

Top: These butt-joined chestnut boards in a cheaply constructed chest have separated. Someone has tried to fill the cracks with putty, to no avail. *Bottom:* These tongue- and- groove-joined oak boards in a tabletop show virtually no separation; the boards are effectively locked together.

Glued-up Parts

Just as tabletops may be glued-up from several boards to form a wide, flat surface, so the legs of chests, tables, and chairs are often made from more than one piece of wood, especially legs that vary greatly in thickness. How is that possible? Well, consider a table leg: If it is turned, the largest diameter of the leg might be 2 1/4 inches, but the main stem of the leg might be only 1 1/4 inches. In such a case, glued-on blocks of wood might be applied to the area where 2 1/4 inches are required. The result, after turning, will be a leg that, upon close examination of its thickest point, will appear to be made of slices of wood—much like those of a hard-boiled egg after it has been cut with a wire egg slicer.

Those may curl and separate, especially if the piece is not stripped carefully. In addition, even legs that are not turned may be pieced together, as may also be the back posts of chairs. The important thing to remember is that whenever you can spot such glued-up parts, be aware that they are usually far weaker than the same parts made of solid wood.

Critical Points and Joints

A critical point is where a piece of furniture is likely to be stressed the most. And as with human joints, if one furniture joint is weakened or impaired, the rest must bear the brunt. In the best furniture, not only are good joints used at critical points, but the joints themselves may get a little extra bracing.

Most pieces of furniture have only one or two critical points, and it's in your best interest to check them out. If you find a piece that is already broken at a critical point, or has been repaired there before, you may be buying a problem best left to someone else.

Chairs. The critical point is the junction of the seat and the back posts. Leaning back in any chair—especially a high-back one—turns the back of the chair into a cantilever (figure 14). Therefore, the best side chairs are those that have braces in the form of ample slats, splats, or spindles, which help to distribute the stresses over a larger area. The best armchairs have arms that extend close to

Figure 14

A critical point in a chair is where the seat frame is joined to the back posts. Although this particular joint uses two dowels, it still shows signs of separation due to strain and glue deterioration.

Figure 15

This chair has a commonly found curved brace screwed into the seat frame and back posts at the critical point, but the brace itself is cracking in its center, and the break is impossible to repair effectively.

Figure 16

A view of the interior rear corner of a well-constructed chest of drawers. The top is properly screwed down (note the long screw holes in the rear), and there's a full dustboard separating the drawers and also a corner block.

Figure 17

The drawer separators in this chest of drawers have been joined to the case with open dovetails, an excellent construction method.

the front of the seat and as high as possible in back.

The same cantilever action occurs where the arms meet the back posts, so check those points as well. Also, twisting around in a framed-seat chair creates a corkscrewlike motion, and unless there are corner braces under the seat to restrain it, the motion will be transmitted to the entire chair. For the same reasons, rungs between chair legs always make for a sturdier chair.

Tables. On most tables the critical point is where the legs join the apron. If the legs are both too spindly and lack cross bracing near the bottom, merely brushing against the table will cause the legs to flex and spring back, eventually harming the critical joints. Corner blocks under the top or stretchers between the legs help to minimize this.

On pedestal tables unevenly distributed weight can turn the tops into seesaws, but since the connection between the top and the center pedestal is usually stronger than the joining of the legs to the pedestal, the legs may become loose or break out completely at their joints.

Case pieces. In relatively heavy pieces that are raised on legs, the critical point is the joining of the case and the legs. Case pieces are always top heavy and become more so with the added weight of books, dishes, and the like. Case pieces also have a tendency to become "unsquare" as they list to one side or the other. Corner blocks under the top, in the corners, and at the bottom of the case will help stop these tendencies (figure 16). So also will horizontal dividers between drawers that are dovetailed in place rather than simply butted in (figure 17). Dustboards between drawers will help even more.

While you're at it, check the back of the case piece. If the back is made of thin plywood that has begun to delaminate—an indication that the piece has been stored in a damp area—you may have to replace the back.

Ideally, all wooden furniture should be constructed so **The Last Word** that all the parts can expand or contract at the same time or so that they can move independently of each other. That's not much of a problem with chairs but can present difficulties with case pieces. For example, if the top, bottom, two sides, and shelves of a bookcase are made of the same wood, seasoned in the same way, all the parts will shrink or expand at the same rate. However, if the bottom is made of plywood or of any other relatively stable material, the sides may split.

The same thing will happen to a sideboard with a solid top that is rigidly fastened to plywood sides, or to a dining table with a solid top immovably attached to the aprons. In good-quality furniture, therefore, the tops are not glued or nailed down but are instead attached with screws, clips, or blocks (figure 16). You will usually find these by looking under the tops. The screw holes will be elongated so that the screws can ride back and forth, and the clips or blocks will be designed to fit into grooves.

Any piece of furniture, regardless of age, that you feel hesitant to use, that trembles to the touch, that you approach with trepidation, will either be useless or short lived. But there are many pieces of all periods and styles that can please the eye and still be serviceable. The best are those pieces whose drawers run so smoothly that they can be closed simply by pushing at one corner, or whose cupboard doors have been fitted so snugly that before they are closed, the air in the cabinet must be let out.

The pinnacle of perfection, the yardstick of quality in furniture making, is the piano. Should you find a piece on which the same care has been lavished as on a piano, you will know you have found something of quality.

4

THE FROSTING ON THE CASE: ORNAMENTATION AND HARDWARE

THE NICE THING about the used-furniture market is that there's something for everyone—not only in the overall designs of furniture but in the furniture's ornamentation as well. If you favor leaves and lion heads, cupids and curlicues, they're waiting for you somewhere. Or perhaps you're thoroughly modern; you like cleaner, less cluttered designs, and there's that, too. Finally, there's the in-between: rounded corners with just a tad of carving or molding.

In this chapter we'll take a look at several types of ornamentation you're likely to find on used furniture. Ornamentation is important to know about because, as with wood and construction, the quality of a piece's ornamentation can bespeak the quality of the rest of it.

Carving

Ornamental furniture-carving is a specialized trade. When it was done by hand, a carver—not a cabinetmaker—took on the task. When the machine age prevailed, companies sprang up that did nothing but make and sell carvings and small turnings to the furniture companies. At flea markets I've seen boxes and boxes containing thousands of identical loose carvings that never found their way to a piece of furniture.

Carving falls into different categories. Wood may be carved away from the surface surrounding the carving to form a high relief pattern, although this is somewhat rare; wood may be chiseled away so that the carving itself is

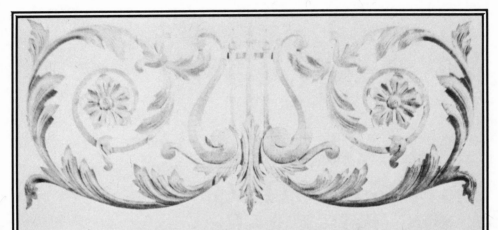

Novelty Wood Works

97 and 99 SIXTH STREET.
GRAND RAPIDS, MICH.

WE MANUFACTURE

CARVINGS

FOR

**Furniture Manufacturers, School and Church Furniture
Manufacturers and for all others that use
Carving for Decorating.**

YOUR ORDERS RESPECTFULLY SOLICITED.

Figure 18

Opposite: Novelty Wood Works was only one of many companies that did nothing but manufacture carvings. (*The Grand Rapids Furniture Record,* 1900)

in relief but does not protrude beyond the surface of the wood; wood may be incised so that the carving is below the surface. Carving may be full round or half round, or, most common of all, it may simply be glued onto the surface but not be a part of it.

Hand Carving. This requires time, effort, and skill, so don't expect to find much true hand carving on mass-produced, used furniture. Hand carving can often be detected by little imperfections and a slight asymmetry in design, which are, in effect, the "signatures" of the carver. Hand carvers try to achieve the sharpest results possible and must use expensive, hard woods to get it: mahogany, walnut, cherry, and the like.

Machine Carving. This is what you're likely to find on used furniture (figures 19–23). It's done with high-speed rotary cutters that descend into the wood vertically, not unlike a dentist's drill. In conjunction with a pantograph-

Figure 19

A full-round carving on the leg of a Golden Oak pedestal table. Machine carving of this quality is fairly rare. (The complete table is shown in figure 60.)

Figure 20

This high-relief shell pattern at the crest of a headboard has been carved directly from the oak, whereas the lower carving (partially visible) has been glued onto the quarter-sawed oak veneer. Note the striations ("flashes") in the veneer in the lower section and the fact that the grain runs in two different directions.

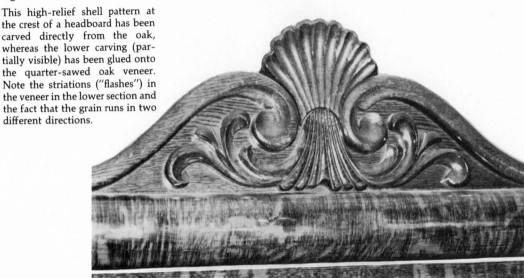

Figure 21

Glued-on (applied) carving at the top of a mirror frame on a chest of drawers.

like device, the rotary cutters follow a pattern that was originally hand-carved. But since the rotary cutters remove wood by chewing it up rather than by chiseling it away cleanly, machine carving is usually not as sharp in outline as hand carving. Although machine carving may sometimes be finished by hand, that, too, requires the kind of extra time and care that would be lavished only on good furniture made of good woods.

Figure 22

Although this lion's head carved at the end of a chair crest-rail is fairly shallow, the design is lively and effective.

Figure 23

Although cut directly from the wood, this carving in a sofa back is in much lower relief than that in figure 20.

Simulated Carving

Basically, there are two types of simulated carving: pressed and molded.

Pressed Ornament. Almost everyone has heard of pressed-back chairs. They're the ones with designs on their backs that are fairly elaborate but not particularly deep or sharp (figure 24). This process of embossing designs with heavy presses into oak and other woods is

Figure 24

A shallow, embossed pattern in the crest rail of a pressed-back chair.

quick, easy, and cheap. Thus furniture with embossed designs is often not of the highest quality. But such pieces are popular, easy to resell, and may be quite attractive.

Molded Ornament. The practice of casting ornaments in a mold and then gluing them onto furniture is centuries old. The material used may be wood based—anglypta, for example, which is molded or pressed wood-pulp—or may be plaster or even terra-cotta.

Molded ornaments are sometimes quite deceptive and difficult to distinguish from hand carving. This is so because the mold is made from an original hand carving, and the casting is very true to the original, often including the idiosyncracies of handwork and even the wood pores. Moreover, when molded ornaments are applied to furniture that has a natural finish, the ornament is painted to match the grain and color of the surrounding wood. In many cases the painting is so faithful to the natural background that the only way to determine if the molding is

Figure 25
A high-quality, solid-brass drawer pull on an Art Nouveau table. The key for the lock is still in place. (The complete table is shown in figure 44.)

"real" is to scratch away a little of the surface paint. On the other hand, if the furniture is factory painted instead of naturally finished, you can almost always assume that the "carvings" are in reality molded ornament.

Sawed Ornament

Sawed ornament appears in wooden grilles behind the glass doors of secretaries, the bands of "carving" around the aprons of tables in a Greek key design or filigree, the filigree cutout brackets on whatnot shelves, or between the tops and legs of occasional tables. On cheaper furniture all of these will have been stamped or sawed from extremely thin plywood and applied to the furniture with glue. If the furniture has to be stripped, nine times out of ten the plywood will delaminate, or the ornament will fall off, or—worse—both.

Hardware

The knobs, hinges, pulls, brackets, galleries, and finials on furniture may be ornamental (exposed) or purely functional (usually hidden) or both. If any of this hardware is

Figure 26

Note the broken hat hook on this Golden Oak hall stand. Finding an exact duplicate will be very difficult, and the only alternative is to replace all the hooks. Current price: $300–$400.

obviously cheaply made—is tinny, rusty, or badly pitted —the furniture on which it has been mounted will probably not be any better. But don't lump merely tarnished hardware in this category: Some of the best metals tarnish —for example, good, solid brass. One way you can detect solid brass is with a magnet: It won't adhere.

Should any of the hardware—exposed or concealed, good or cheap—be missing or malfunctioning, you'll have a hard time replacing it. Almost all hardware has been specially designed for and by the manufacturer, and much of it is patented. It cannot simply be matched with the stuff you find in your local hardware store.

If one drawer pull is missing, it probably means that all the pulls will have to be replaced; at least you should be able to find something you like among the many types on the market, some of which are reproductions made by specialty manufacturers. However, the purely functional hardware is rarely replaceable. An extension-table slide or the mechanism on desks that automatically extends the support slides for the writing surface will probably have been made for a specific table or desk. A longer or shorter piece of hardware, scavenged from another piece of furniture, can seldom be adapted to your needs. Replacement functional hardware may have to be custom made.

So when you buy furniture that has movable parts, make sure all the parts are there and functioning properly. In particular, pull out extension tables to their full length (and while you're at it, make sure all the leaves are there and that they match and fit and have not themselves been scavenged from other tables). See that you have matching bedrails and that the metal hooks at the ends fit into the head- and footboards correctly. Check to see that locks have keys and that the hinges on drop-leaf tables are not broken and the wood around the screws not split out.

A thorough check of hardware will save you a wild-goose chase for parts that are difficult or impossible to come by.

PART TWO

5

TROUBLESHOOTING:
REPAIRING, REVIVING, AND REFINISHING USED FURNITURE

Used Furniture

THERE'S A SHAGGY-DOG STORY about a dog, which goes on and on as shaggy-dog stories will, but eventually the dog in the story dies from eating a can of varnish. The poor dog met a terrible end, of course, but he had a great finish!

Much used furniture had at least a good finish when it left the factory, but some of that furniture has met a terrible end, too. It's dead, and no amount of artificial respiration is likely to revive it.

Fortunately, however, most used furniture can be easily repaired, revived, and, if necessary, refinished. And if you do the work yourself, you're going to save money—first, because a piece of furniture that is in the rough, that needs some work, always costs less to buy than the same piece already restored by someone else; and second, because your investment in supplies, added to the base cost, will rarely exceed the dealer's tacked-on charge for his own, or subcontracted, work. The only caveat here is that you may have to make an investment in tools, but for simple work you won't need many.

Before reviving the finish of a piece, or completely refinishing it, you'll need to do any necessary repairs so we'll start with that.

Simple Repairs

For several reasons, I'm going to give you some hints only about relatively simple repairs to furniture. For one thing, I don't think that used furniture requiring extensive structural repairs is worth buying. There's simply too much of it around that is in reasonably good shape to justify the time and effort required to put a broken-down hulk back on its feet, both literally and figuratively. Also, most people don't own the tools necessary for extensive repairs. Finally, whole books have already been written on the subject of repairs, and I don't have the space to delve into the subject in detail.

Incidentally, the glue I recommend for most of your wood repairs is the aliphatic resin variety. It's light brown, sometimes labeled "Professional," and is sold in the same sort of translucent plastic squeeze bottles that the traditional white glue is packaged in. The latter is also acceptable and somewhat less expensive. In some cases you may also need clear epoxy glue, silicon adhesive, or contact cement.

The following, then, is a troubleshooter's guide to some of the problems you may encounter and how to solve them quickly.

Sticking Drawer. Rub the edges of the drawer with paraffin or spray with graphite. If that doesn't work, put the drawer in a warm oven for a few hours to shrink the wood. If that fails, you'll have to plane down the edges slightly.

Drawer Falling Apart. Pull out all loose parts or knock them apart with a rubber-faced hammer. (A steel hammer covered with a cloth is also suitable.) Scrape out the old glue with a knife and recoat the surfaces lightly with aliphatic glue. Reassemble the drawer and clamp it with a tourniquet. To do this, wrap a cord around the drawer loosely, knot it, then make a loop. Insert a stick in the loop and twist it until the cord is tight. Put the stick in the drawer to prevent the cord from loosening. An even simpler tourniquet can be made from those nylon tie-down straps used to hold car-top carriers.

Bottom of Drawer Cracked. This is an "optional" repair, as the bottom probably won't fall out. Separate the crack slightly, dab in epoxy glue, then tap the bottom back together with a rubber hammer until the crack is closed up. Wipe off excess glue.

Knobs or Handles Loose. First, try tightening the knob with a screwdriver. If it doesn't hold, remove the bolt or screw holding the knob, coat it with silicon adhesive, and retighten. In a day or two check for tightness, and if the knob is slightly loose, tighten it down a little more. As an alternative with wooden knobs, you can insert a thicker or longer screw rather than use adhesive.

Door or Fall-Front Desk Lid Falling Off Due to Loose Hinges. If the hinge is broken, you'll have to replace it. If the screws holding the hinges have stripped the threads in the wood, try driving in a slightly longer wood screw. If that doesn't work, insert wood putty in the original screw holes and let dry. Then drill a very narrow hole in the dry putty and redrive the old screws.

Rocking-Chair Rocker Cracked. Pull the crack apart, coat with epoxy glue, and reassemble. If possible, clamp the break with a C-clamp, or tourniquet the chair legs, until the glue sets.

Loose or Wobbly Legs. Check the reason for the wobble or looseness, which will probably occur at a critical joint.

If the piece is a pedestal table, you will have to remove the legs, scrape out the old glue, and then reassemble using aliphatic glue.

If the originally screwed-down corner blocks in a chair or table are loose and the threads in the wood are stripped so the screws cannot be retightened, remove the old screws and insert longer ones, tightening them down.

If the wobble is due to loose stretchers or rungs, try knocking the legs apart with a rubber hammer. Clean out the old glue with a knife and reassemble with aliphatic glue. If the piece cannot be knocked apart completely, pull it apart as far as possible. Then drill a very narrow hole into the leg through the joint. Inject the joint with glue

Figure 27

Heavy black lines indicate the placement of quarter-inch dowels in the stretchers and seat frame of a late-1930s oak chair.

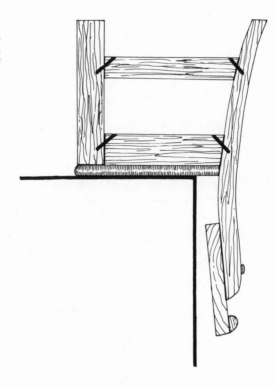

through the hole, using a hypodermic needle or a special glue injector (see your hardware store). Pound the piece back together, wiping up any excess glue. Use a tourniquet to clamp the legs.

However, if you can manage it, by far the best way to tighten wobbly stretchers, and legs that are loose at the seat frame, is to drill quarter-inch holes at a forty-five-degree angle through the frame into the rear legs, or through the rungs into the legs (figure 27). Then take a quarter-inch dowel and insert it into one of the holes you've drilled to test for length. Whittle the end of the dowel slightly with a knife and saw off the dowel to the proper length. Apply aliphatic glue to the dowel and inside the hole, and hammer the dowel into the hole. Repeat the process for the other holes, wiping up any excess glue.

Chair Arm Loose. Check the reason for this. Wooden plugs or buttons directly behind the point of attachment of the arm and the seat back may conceal loose screws. Pry out the buttons with a knife or screwdriver, or drill out the wooden plugs. Now try tightening the screws. If that doesn't work, remove the screws and replace them with longer screws. Replace the buttons, insert dowels into the screw holes, or, as a last resort, plug the holes with wood putty and stain to match the color of the chair.

In many cases, arms that are loose where they meet the arm supports can be tapped apart with a rubber hammer and then reassembled with aliphatic glue.

Piece Is Unstable Because One Leg Is Too Short. The simplest but least elegant way of fixing this is with wood putty. First, set the piece on a very flat, even surface (for example, a piece of plywood). Place a couple of table-spoons of wood putty on a square of aluminum foil or waxed paper, insert in under the short leg, and gently press the leg into the wood putty, cleaning away as much excess around the leg as possible. After the putty has set, shape it to the contours of the leg with a file or sandpaper and stain it to match.

The best method to cure instability, though, is to set the piece on the plywood with the longest leg near the edge. Using a wood saw that is flat against the plywood, carefully saw off the end of the longest leg one sawblade thickness. Continue this process until the piece is stable.

Loose Veneer. Scrape out the old glue under the veneer with a knife. Squirt a little aliphatic glue under the veneer and press down, wiping up any excess glue that oozes out. Then cover the veneer with waxed paper and weight it down with something heavy until the glue dries.

Blistered or Wavy Veneer. Try this first: Cover the dam-aged veneer with a piece of lint-free cloth and place a clothes iron at its lowest setting on the cloth. Leave the iron in place for six to eight hours. You may find that the veneer has re-adhered by itself. If it hasn't, and the veneer is brittle, you'll have to soften it. Do this with a dampened lint-free cloth and the clothes iron set at medium, allow-ing the moisture in the cloth to soften the veneer some-what. (Check the veneer frequently to make sure it is not being damaged and the cloth is not sticking to it.) Then make three cuts in the veneer with a razor blade to form a flap—two cuts with the grain and one across. Lift the flap gently and clean out the old glue and dirt from under the veneer. Then follow the steps above under "Loose Veneer."

Table- or Chest-Top Board Separated. With a knife, scrape the old glue and dirt from between the boards as much as possible. Squeeze aliphatic glue into the joints and clamp together with a heavy tourniquet. If you're using a tourniquet with a stick—as opposed to a nylon tie-down strap—place the stick under the tabletop and use a nail tapped into the underside of the top to keep the tourniquet from loosening. If a tourniquet is impractical or if it doesn't hold well enough, you'll have to invest in (or, preferably, borrow) what's called a pipe clamp. Your hardware dealer will know what it is, and the instructions are on the box.

Rolltop Desk Lid, or Similar Slatted Door, Is Stiff or Broken. This is probably due to the canvas backing becoming dried out or detached from the slats. To cure this, you'll first have to remove the desk lid or door from the piece. Then peel away the canvas from the slats, using a solvent like turpentine if necessary. Next, line up all the slats on a flat surface. Now cut a piece of solid canvas to the size of the lid or door, or use individual strips of canvas carpet-tape cut to the proper length, one piece of tape for every three or four inches in width of the lid or door. Coat the lid or door with contact cement and do the same to the canvas. Following the directions on the bottle or can of cement, allow the cement to dry slightly, then carefully lay the canvas or carpet-tape strips in place across the slats. Do it right the first time because it will be difficult to adjust the canvas or tape if you make a mistake. Now press the canvas or tape all over for a good bond, and allow the cement to cure for a day or two before reassembling the piece.

Solid Brass Is Tarnished. Of course, any piece of solid brass can be burnished with the usual brass-polishing products. But if the tarnished surface is large—say, a brass bed—using brass polish will be extremely time consuming, not to mention expensive.

To cut your work by about one third, follow this method, which is preferably done out of doors. First, check the piece to determine if it is coated with lacquer that has deteriorated and allowed the brass to tarnish, which is almost certainly the case. Remove the lacquer with lacquer thinner or acetone.

Next you will have to rub down the piece with old rags and muriatic acid. This substance, which is available in hardware stores, is diluted hydrochloric acid. Needless to say, it's dangerous even when diluted, so you'd do well to wear goggles to protect your eyes as well as rubber gloves for your hands. A great deal of the black tarnish will come off on your rags.

Now hose down the piece with water and let it dry thoroughly. Then use your brass polish to get a mirrorlike sheen. If you wish, seal the finish with liquid (not spray-can) lacquer, carefully applied with a brush made for use with lacquer. The lacquer will dry very quickly.

Mirror Is Tarnished or Spotty. Any mirror can be replaced, of course, but that is not advisable, especially with good, early beveled-glass mirrors. Instead, I recommend that you have a professional resilver the mirror. Doing it yourself in the old way—with genuine tin foil and mercury—is a complex and tedious process. I've heard that there is a new kit on the market that simplifies the process for the do-it-yourselfer, but I haven't had much luck in tracking it down. Perhaps you will.

Revive or Refinish?

Now that you've done your minor repairs, it's time to think about going to work on the piece's finish. I've already told you my point of view about old furniture finishes, but I think it bears repeating. I feel very strongly that, if at all possible, the original finish of a piece should be preserved, and this for several reasons.

First, historically all furniture still bearing its original finish has inevitably become worth more than refinished pieces, and I haven't noticed any indication that this trend is going to change. Second, I'm lazy, and it's easier for me to revive a finish than it is to completely redo a piece. And finally, I think that things should look the way they were intended to look. I wouldn't paint a New England saltbox house hot pink any more than I would turn a piece of furniture that was originally dark and varnished into a piece that is light and oil-finished.

If you disagree with me, that's fine, but remember that you are investing your money in your furniture, and completely refinishing a piece may be tantamount to using hundred-dollar bills to start a campfire.

Reviving an Old Finish

An old finish may be dirty, dull, faded, spotted, alligatored, and more, but those problems can usually be dealt with very handily. Here's how.

Testing the Finish. This is always the first step, for each type of finish—shellac, lacquer, or varnish—must be treated differently. When testing the finish, always do it in an inconspicuous part of the piece of furniture.

Test for shellac with denatured alcohol, sometimes sold as shellac thinner. Rub the finish with a clean cloth. If the finish dissolves, it's shellac.

If nothing happens, try lacquer thinner or acetone. If the finish softens and dissolves, it's lacquer.

If that doesn't work, the finish is almost certainly varnish. If necessary, this can be tested with any commercial paint-remover.

Cleaning the Finish. Sometimes a good cleaning is all it takes to perk up an old finish. Try any or all of the following methods, beginning in an inconspicuous spot, but do not use a water-based cleaner on a shellac finish since it may turn the finish white. Also, before any cleaning, reviving, or refinishing, always remove any ornamental hardware from the piece.

If built-up wax seems to be the problem, it can easily be removed with turpentine. Denatured alcohol can also be used on varnished surfaces.

An excellent all-purpose cleaner can be made from a

three-to-one mixture of turpentine and boiled linseed oil. (The can will be labeled "boiled"; don't try to boil it yourself or you may go up in flames.) Apply the cleaner with a lint-free cloth and/or 000 steel wool, rubbing with the grain. Then wipe down the piece again with another cloth.

If that doesn't work to your satisfaction, try using a mild detergent and water. Dishwashing liquid is fine.

Reviving the Finish. If your test indicates a shellac finish, here's what to do. Get a clean jar and into it measure two parts of paraffin oil to one part of white shellac. If you can't get paraffin oil, substitute olive oil. Mix thoroughly. Use a lint-free cloth or 000 steel wool to rub down the piece with the grain. Then wipe down the piece again.

For varnish finishes, you'll need a different mixture—a combination of three parts turpentine to one part *raw* (as opposed to boiled) linseed oil. Follow the same procedure as with the shellac reviver.

It is sometimes possible to revive a lacquer finish by rubbing a piece down with FFF pumice or rottenstone. Follow the directions on the box.

White Spots and Water Rings. These can usually be successfully removed with cigarette or cigar ashes and salad oil. Dip a cloth or a cork in the oil, then in the ashes, then rub with the grain across the white spot. Keep rubbing and dipping and rubbing. The ashes should act as a mild abrasive, and the spot should disappear.

It didn't work? Then try salad oil and table salt. If that doesn't work, try oil and rottenstone or FFF pumice.

I understand that there are also commercial products specifically made for white-spot removal, but I've never had to use one and don't know if they work.

Scratches. Believe it or not, nutmeats rubbed into scratches often darken them enough to obliterate them. Try broken pieces of walnuts, pecans, or Brazil nuts. You can always eat the leftover nuts if the process isn't as effective as you'd like.

Next, try rubbing the scratches with a little raw linseed

oil. Finally, try some of the commercial scratch-covering products: the crayonlike stick shellacs sold in paint and hardware stores, or the furniture polish-stain combinations. Follow the directions.

Burns. Rub down the burn with 000 steel wool and wipe clean with denatured alcohol until the burned area lightens in color somewhat. Then fill the resulting depression with stick lacquer or shellac of a color that matches the piece's finish.

Checking or Alligatoring. A checked surface is one with a fine network of lines running through it, caused by shrinking of varnish. Alligatoring is like checking only worse and is thus more difficult to restore. What you'll need in any case is a well-ventilated area (outdoors is the best-ventilated area I know of) and a can of benzol or a commercial "amalgamator." Ask your hardware- or paint-store clerk for it.

Generally speaking, all you have to do is lightly brush down the damaged finish with the amalgamator until it smooths out. Let the piece alone for twenty-four hours and the varnish will reharden. Then rub down the piece with oil and FFF pumice. Finish off the job with paste wax, if you'd like.

Dents. The classic method of removing dents—preferably shallow ones—is to steam them out. But don't use this method on shellac finishes.

First, remove only the finish covering the dent. Use a small amount of paint remover for this. Then dampen a lint-free cloth and hold a hot clothes iron against the cloth and the dent, checking every minute or so to see if the dented wood has swelled out. Eventually, of course, you'll reach a point where the wood cannot absorb any more moisture, and the dent will have been swelled out as much as possible. Let the spot dry for twenty-four hours.

Next, you may have to restain the treated spot. Do this with a stain that seems to match the original color, but thinned out a little. Keep applying stain until the colors match, then revarnish the dent. If the new varnish is obtrusive after it has dried, mix some amalgamator with denatured alcohol in a one-to-one ratio and use the mixture to carefully blend in the new varnish with the old. (For more information on stains and varnishes, see the section on "The New Finish," below.)

Bare Spots. In areas where the finish has worn through, follow the method above, but, of course, omit the iron and the damp cloth.

Ink Stains. Here I usually admit defeat. An ink spot that has penetrated through the finish to the wood is, as far as I have been able to determine, impossible to remove. You'll probably just have to live with it. If the ink has not penetrated too deeply, it may be possible to remove it using ammonia or oxalic acid, both of which will have a bleaching effect. Or try rubbing down the stain with oil and FFF pumice, and clean up with turpentine.

Leather Tops. Genuine leather tops are usually found only on good furniture. If the leather is dirty, it can be washed with saddle soap. Cracked or dried-out leather can be rejuvenated with neat's-foot oil. But leather tops that are burned or stained will have to be replaced unless you can live with them that way. That goes for leather tops that have been painted to *hide* burns and stains, as well.

Stripping

You've thrown in the towel; you can't save the original finish. Perhaps it has a layer or two of paint over it, or it's so alligatored that no amalgamator will salvage it. You've decided to have the piece stripped, or to strip it yourself, and then to refinish it. But before you do—and before we delve into that subject—let me inject a few words of caution.

First, you'll remember my mentioning in Chapter 3 that the tops of many pieces—chests and tables, for example—may consist of anywhere from three to five narrow boards glued together, perhaps even more. Now, since these boards may come from different parts of a log, or even from different trees, the color and grain of the boards rarely if ever matched. They were therefore skilfully blended at the factory with stains and finishes to achieve a uniform appearance. So if the solid-wood furniture you bought is going to be stripped and refinished, you'd better add in the cost of matching and blending the new finish.

In addition, woods that have a uniform, bland grain were often stained and finished by the manufacturer to simulate such rarer woods as mahogany or walnut. The person with an unpracticed eye, who sees only the color but does not look closely at the pores or grain, might be fooled, indeed, might even fancy the harsh red or brown stains. Others, who prefer their furniture more mellow and natural, might buy the piece with an eye to getting it stripped. I'll apply a nice, smooth coat of satin-finish varnish, or perhaps I'll just wax it so as not to hide the natural wood—that's the thought. Well, think again. Stripping will indeed remove the finish, but underneath you're likely to find a stain that, thanks to modern chemistry, is practically ineradicable. Strong bleaches will seem to remove some of the stains, but the color will always strike through again. This is perhaps the largest single source of disappointment to the buyer of used furniture, and the only way to avoid it is to know your woods.

Veneered pieces can create even more problems than those made of solid woods. The veneered parts will usually be the large, flat surfaces—tabletops, chest tops and sides, drop fronts on desks, drawers and doors on any given piece. On the other hand, the supporting parts—pedestals, legs, and frames, for example—will very likely be of solid wood. The prominent veneered parts will, furthermore, be such fine woods as mahogany, walnut, or cherry, while the solid parts may be of lesser, cheaper woods stained and finished to match the veneer. The result after stripping?

● A beautiful mahogany dining-table top combined with an almost white base.

● A secretary with a mahogany writing surface and

drawer fronts, but doors, sides, front frame, and legs
a splotchy purplish color.
- An inlaid walnut-burl pedestal-table top with a
  tattletale-gray base.

The list could go on. And unless you like your furniture
multicolored, you'll be faced with an expensive color-
matching job.

Furthermore, you should carefully check *all* veneered
furniture made roughly between 1920 and 1940. During
that period it was discovered that the old, reliable animal
glues, which had to be applied hot, were too difficult to
use in the mass production of veneered furniture. However, a glue made from the milk by-product casein, which
could be applied cold and could be easily spread by machine, seemed perfect, and by the 1920s most manufacturers were using it. But what no one realized at the time
was that the casein glue, after a period of years, became
vulnerable to a fungus that would cause it to deteriorate
and cause the veneer to delaminate.

For that reason you should know how to identify not
only veneered furniture in general but also those veneered
pieces on which casein glue has been used, since the latter
can be double trouble. Here are some tips:
- Examine the back edges of the top of a chest or the
  edges of a drawer and you will be able to detect the
  veneered facing, since the edges of the cores on even
  the best furniture are not themselves hidden behind
  veneers.
- The tops of chests and tables that are very uniform
  in grain and color and that have evenly spaced joints
  are probably veneered.
- So are case pieces that have no overhanging tops,
  or that have no break between the tops and the sides,
  or that have a grain on the tops that matches the
  grain on the sides.
- Any surface may be veneered where the wood
  grain forms a distinct design or where more than one
  wood is present.
- Drawer fronts that are curved or that have a vertical grain pattern are probably veneered.

• To identify casein-glued pieces, first check the exposed surfaces: hairline cracks, loose veneers near the edges, and blisters are obvious signs of a failing bond; also, sniff the piece, and if you detect a strong, mildewlike odor, pass it up.

There are veneered pieces that show no evidence of delamination that still might give you a problem. For if the stripping solution gets between the veneer and the core, the glue may let go and the veneer may come off in sheets (radio and gramophone cabinets seem to be particularly vulnerable to this). Therefore, before stripping any of this furniture, test a small, inconspicuous area with paint remover. If the veneer loosens, it may be better to sand off the finish very lightly with number 240 or 320 silicon carbide paper (see "Sanding," below), or soften the finish gradually and carefully with the proper solvent (see "Testing the Finish," above). Remember, too, that the veneer may be only 1/64-inch thick!

Finally, think twice about even buying furniture that has been painted or "antiqued" by an amateur, as opposed to a factory. For one thing, the paint may be concealing serious structural or surface damage. For example, a Golden Oak dining chair was probably never painted except to hide damage. The damage could have been caused by a leaky attic, or by someone carving his initials into the seat, but no matter, the chair was painted to hide it. I've seen claw-foot pedestal tables freshly painted to hide the fact that some of the missing toes or a whole foot have been simulated with plaster. The paint can be removed easily, but the plaster foot will remain. All furniture that has been painted—especially recently—is suspect. It will rarely yield beautiful, natural woods. If you are buying from a dealer, tell him that you will plunk down your money only *after* you've seen the piece stripped.

Commercial Dip-Stripping. There are two types of commercial stripping, sometimes found in the same shop: the hot-tank method and the cold-tank method.

A hot tank contains 140° F caustic soda. Furniture

dipped into it must be neutralized after stripping. Then the furniture can be thrown away. Why? Because hot-tank stripping loosens joints, raises grain, loosens veneer, delaminates plywood, warps boards . . . you get the idea. Don't let anyone talk you into hot-tank stripping. The only thing it's good for is metal, shutters, ceramics, and possibly solid-wood doors.

The cold-tank method is more acceptable but, alas, more expensive, because the chemicals cost more than caustic soda. If done correctly—if the piece is not left in the tank too long and is washed down afterward—cold-tank stripping is appropriate for all used furniture except delicate, veneered pieces. It's also a time-saving method for pieces with lots of intricate, narrow turnings or with deep carvings that are hard to reach. Even so, proper cold-tank stripping may not remove every last trace of paint, and you may have to do some hand stripping.

Choosing a stripper is like choosing a doctor: get a referral, if you can, from someone else who's used the stripper and who is satisfied with the stripper's work.

Do-It-Yourself Stripping. No doubt about it, hand-stripping of varnished or painted furniture is a smelly, messy, tedious business, and I have yet to meet anyone who considered it even vaguely amusing. For the satisfaction in a job well done comes later—sometimes a lot later —when your newly refinished piece of furniture is completely fixed up and in place and you can sit back and enjoy it. On the other hand, do-it-yourself stripping isn't particularly difficult, so why not give it a try if you're really interested in saving money?

First, you'll need paint remover. You may as well start with the cheapest stuff you can find, which will probably be a liquid as opposed to a semipaste or jelly; the liquids usually work faster and have no wax thickeners to clog up the wood pores. However, if you're working on chairs or intricate carvings, the semipastes may be better because they cling to the surface of the piece. You'll also need the following: an old or inexpensive paintbrush (and possibly a toothbrush for intricate areas); burlap and/or 00 steel wool; rags; newspapers; empty cans; some old clothes (especially shoes); rubber gloves (make sure they're neoprene); and a well-ventilated area.

Here's what to do. First, remove all the ornamental hardware from the piece. Pour your paint remover into an empty can, brush it onto the piece, and allow it to soak in just enough to soften the paint or varnish. If there are several coats of paint, try to wait until the paint remover has penetrated them all; test for softness with the end of your toothbrush or with an ice-cream-bar stick; but don't leave the remover on too long or the paint or varnish may reharden.

Next, with your putty knife strip off as much of the old finish as possible. Use your newspapers to wipe down the putty knife after each pass. Use your steel wool and/or burlap to get into cracks and crevices and also to wipe down large, flat surfaces (with the grain, needless to say).

You may have to do all of the above two or three times to achieve a good, clean job. When you have, wipe down the whole piece with rags and/or 00 steel wool and turpentine, and let it sit and dry for a day. You're done!

The New Finish

Now this part can be fun. I, at least, enjoy it because I know the stripping ordeal is over. I told you I was lazy.

Here are most of the items you'll need for your new finish. You may use all of them or just a few, depending on what sort of finish you're after, but I'll list them all anyway: waterproof silicon carbide sandpaper, emery cloth, a three-by-five-inch rubber-faced sanding block, a tack rag, good brushes, steel wool, wood fillers, stains, turpentine, an oil-finish product, and varnish. Your hardware- or paint-store person will know what each of those items is.

Sanding. A good final finish requires a smooth surface, and to achieve that you'll need good abrasive paper. In fact, you'll need two types in different grades: several sheets of numbers 180, 240, and 320 "grit" waterproof silicon carbide paper, plus some sheets of emery cloth in various grades of fineness. The former are for flat surfaces, the latter for turnings and carvings. If you do not intend to do very fine work, you may not need the number 320 silicon carbide paper. The less expensive garnet sandpaper may be substituted for silicon carbide, but it must be used dry and won't last as long.

For large, flat surfaces, fold and tear your number 180 silicon carbide paper to size and attach it to your sanding block. Now wet down the wood surface with turpentine and sand evenly with the grain until you achieve a smooth surface and all the "whiskers" of extraneous wood have been removed. (Note: If you intend to use a wood filler, now is the time, after your first coarse sanding. See the next section, "Filling," below.)

Now wipe down the piece with turpentine and switch to your number 240 paper, following the same procedure as above and using the turp as a cutting fluid. Do the same with the number 320 paper if you're a perfectionist and want to impress your friends and enemies. Use your flexible emery cloth dry for narrow turnings and other intricate work.

Finally, wipe down the piece with a rag and turpentine. The damp surface should give you an idea of what the piece will look like finished naturally rather than stained. If you like that look, well and good. You won't have to stain.

Filling. Wood filler is used to smooth out the surface of coarse, porous woods like oak and chestnut and sometimes walnut and mahogany. As far as I'm concerned, the use of it is optional. That is, porous surfaces don't bother me a particle. But if you demand smoothness—on a tabletop, for example—you'll have to use filler.

Paste filler—often called "silex"—is what you'll need. Vacuum or brush out all the dust in the wood pores, work in the filler and wipe down the piece according to the package directions, let dry, and then continue with your number 240 silicon carbide paper as discussed in the previous section.

Staining. You'll use a stain, of course, only if you wish to change the color of the wood. From applying turpentine to the raw wood, you've already gotten an idea of what the wood will look like with a simple oil or varnish finish. If you want a better idea, pick an inconspicuous spot and apply a little raw or boiled linseed oil. The raw stuff will yield a lighter appearance than the boiled, the former being closer to a varnish finish, the latter more like an oil finish. If you like what you see, skip this section.

But if you still don't like what you see, it's time to buy stains. For the amateur, I recommend the ordinary premixed, oil-based stains sold under various trade names in hardware and paint stores. Somewhere near the stains the store should display a card with wood samples showing how various types of wood look with different stains, or the store may simply have a printed sheet for the same purpose. Both of those are intended to give you only a general idea of what the finished piece will look like. If you're in doubt, start with the lighter-colored stains, since you can always make a piece darker by applying more stain of the same or a darker color, but you'll have a heck of a time making a dark stain lighter.

Here's what to do now. First, rub down your surface with a tack rag, which will pick up all loose dust. Then brush on your stain as evenly as possible, trying not to overlap already stained sections. Let the piece dry for a minute or two, then blend the color with a rag and wipe down the piece. If the color is not right, repeat the process with the same stain or a darker one until you achieve results that please you. You'll almost always have to use at least two coats. Some experts recommend allowing each coat to dry for twenty-four hours, but I've never had ill effects from immediately restaining a piece. Please note here that stained parts where the end grain is exposed— on the long edge of a tabletop, for example—will absorb more stain and hence darken more quickly than flat- or quarter-cut surfaces, so you may want to use less stain on the end grain than on other surfaces.

Now let the piece dry for at least a day, and then you'll be ready to head for the "finish line."

The Oil Finish. This is my favorite finish for all furniture. It's far and away the easiest and most economical to apply and yields a hand-rubbed look with no hand rubbing. It's also a relatively hard finish and can be waxed for extra gloss. It's not for everyone, though.

The paint or hardware store will sell a product calling itself an oil finish, or perhaps an "antique oil finish." It is so easy to use it almost makes me cry. All you have to do is wipe down the piece with your tack rag, and then apply the oil finish rather generously with a cloth. Just wet down the whole piece more or less evenly, let the finish dry until it's somewhat tacky—say, ten or twenty minutes—then wipe off the excess with another cloth, buffing a little as you merrily roll along.

That's all there is to it. Tabletops, desktops, and similar heavily used surfaces prone to spills and stains are the only ones that will require more than one coat. But the beauty of the oil finish is that you can apply as many coats as you want—with a day's drying time in between, of course—without fear of drips, runs, crawling, or cracking of the finish. For tabletops and the like I recommend three or four coats.

Incidentally, if you want to make certain that the oil doesn't get on your floor or soak through your newspapers, try putting empty tuna-fish or cat-food cans under the feet of the piece.

The Varnish Finish. This is the only other finish you'll want to consider. Shellac is too susceptible to stains, and lacquer too difficult to apply properly unless you have a spray gun.

By *varnish* I mean *polyurethane varnish.* You'll use it if you want an exceedingly tough finish. It comes in glossy, satin, and flat, and you'll have to choose the one that appeals to you most.

First, wipe down your piece with a tack rag. Now, using a good brush made for varnish and at least two inches wide (for large, flat surfaces, at any rate), dip the bristles not more than one third into the varnish and *flow* it onto the surface with the grain. Don't brush too hard (that is, don't make the bristles bend very much); don't brush back and forth; don't brush more than six to eight inches of the surface at a time; do brush with parallel strokes. I should add that on a flat surface it's best to brush from the center to the edges. Table legs and other vertical surfaces are best brushed from the bottom toward the top. But if possible, try to brush all surfaces on the horizontal by turning the piece.

Now, while the varnish is still wet, cross-brush the surface at right angles to your original strokes (that is, brush across the grain). Don't redip your brush into the varnish for this work, but rather use it almost dry. Finish up your work by brushing with the grain again with the brush almost dry.

If you intend to apply another coat, you must allow the first coat to dry for at least twenty-four hours, longer in humid weather. The reason is that you absolutely cannot sand varnish that has not hardened properly. Test for hardness with your fingernail.

For your second coat, rub down the surface lightly with the grain with 000 steel wool or with number 400 silicon carbide paper and turpentine. If you've got any sags or drips, they may be sanded level with number 320 silicon carbide paper—but, I emphasize, *only* if the sags or drips are thoroughly dried. Now go over the surface once again with your tack rag to remove all dust and steel particles and you're ready for a second coat, which should be much easier to apply than the first.

If you're going to be very thorough, you'll varnish the underside of any large, flat surface like a tabletop because it will help to prevent the boards from warping. Let the piece dry, and you're ready to enjoy it and your expert handiwork.

PART THREE

6

SQUARING OFF VICTORIAN:
THE EASTLAKE STYLE, 1872–90

IN 1868 IN ENGLAND, Charles Lock Eastlake published his little book *Hints on Household Taste in Furniture, Upholstery and Other Details.* In 1872—the same year that Montgomery Ward and Company issued its first catalog—*Hints on Household Taste* was published in America, where it became a best-seller, going through eight editions from 1872 to 1890. Indeed, every fashion-conscious family in England and America had a copy of the book, and for a time no one dared redecorate without consulting the words of the master. Even the 1876 Centennial Exposition in Philadelphia was dominated by Eastlake-inspired designs.

Who was the object of all this deference?

Charles Eastlake was an architect and painter who produced his small volume of designs and polemics as a reaction against the French-inspired fussiness of Victorian design and faddishness in general, or, as Eastlake himself put it: "Chairs . . . curved in such a manner as to ensure the greatest amount of ugliness with the least possible comfort" and "this absurd love of change—simply for the sake of change."

Eastlake also despised the increasingly shoddy workmanship in the construction of home furnishings. He urged the good folks of England and America to renounce their expensive, elaborate, overdecorated furniture with its dishonest screws, nails, and glued-on veneers. In ex-

The Historical Background

change, Eastlake offered them a Gothic revival—less expensive, functional, "sincere" chairs, tables, and cupboards devoid of glossy finishes and constructed with wooden pegs and dowels.

A return to Medieval design did not originate with Eastlake. Many people in Victorian England were uncomfortable with the effects of the Industrial Revolution, and several voices had been raised suggesting the adoption of the earlier, simpler English life-style and art forms. Writer, critic, and champion of socialism John Ruskin had organized the Guild of St. George, an elaborate social structure from which machines were virtually banished. And designer William Morris had already begun to create furniture in the Gothic tradition.

But it was Eastlake and his well-illustrated *Hints on Household Taste* that caught the imagination of the public. Eastlake's message was moral as well as esthetic. As far as he was concerned, the style of furniture had as much to do with the "honesty" and "sincerity" of its construction as it did with its overall design. "Simplicity of general form is one of the first conditions of artistic excellence in manufacture," said Eastlake. Moreover, unnecessary ornamentation and veneers bespoke an unwholesome way of life, whereas straight lines and the "natural grain of such woods as oak, rosewood, walnut, &c. . . . not obscured and clogged by artificial varnish" reflected the purity and decency of the owner.

Eastlake also approved the use of inlay and marquetry "where an effect of greater richness is aimed at," as well as shallow carving that had to be done by hand. Honesty of design meant doing away with flimsy hinges for cabinets and bookcases; these were replaced with prominently displayed iron or brass ornamental hardware. Two other Eastlake trademarks were narrow shelves "for displaying the rare china vases and old porcelain" on sideboards and cupboards, and the kinds of turnings that were used extensively on decorative balustrades. As Russell Lynes comments in his book *The Tastemakers,* "Here was a chance not only to redecorate but to be saved at the same time."

Figure 28

The overall squarishness, shallow incised carving, and rosettes near the base are all characteristics of Eastlake-inspired design in this side table. Current price: $100–$250.

Americans had their own reasons for wanting to purify their souls through home furnishings. The country had gone through some transitions. The Civil War was over. The West had been won and was expanding. Industrialization was growing. It was a time of increasing complexity and "progress," yet people hungered for the simplicity of the distant past. In the recent past only the rich had been able to afford good Victorian furniture. Now the growing middle class welcomed the new, imported Eastlake style that was not only within their means but reminded them of a more ordered, less complicated way of life.

Figure 29

Some Eastlake pieces have far more decoration than this chest of drawers has. Current price: $150–$300.

Ironically, however, the straight, relatively simple furniture that had been designed by Eastlake as a reaction against mass production was more easily turned out by machine than its elaborate Victorian predecessors had been. To Eastlake's horror, he discovered that he had created a monster—that the very sort of workmanship he had railed against was now gushing forth from Grand Rapids, and each piece of furniture had some new frill or frippery invented by the manufacturer but still bearing Eastlake's name. For the furniture factories and their subcontractors had no intention of letting their expensive carving, curving, molding, and cutting machinery simply lie idle. Instead, they would crank out furniture that retained the basic squareness of Eastlake's designs and then ornament the pieces with any sorts of flourishes they saw fit. The result was that much American Eastlake furniture was little more than a squared-off version of the elaborate Renaissance revival designs of the 1870–80 period.

In his preface to the fourth edition of *Hints on Household Taste,* Eastlake was prompted to write, "I find American tradesmen continually advertising what they are pleased to call 'Eastlake' furniture, with the production of which I have had nothing whatever to do and for the taste of which I should be very sorry to be considered responsible."

The Current Market

Those of you who have a yen for an authentic Eastlake piece, or one attributed to him, should give up the hunt because there is no such animal. Although he did design some furniture, Eastlake's main role was as a tastemaker. The few pieces that are attributed to him were commissioned by wealthy clients and produced by custom shops, notably Herter Brothers in New York City.

However, you will find many late Victorian pieces that show evidence of the Eastlake influence. They are usually reasonably priced, in part because at the moment the earlier Victorian designs and Golden Oak are more popular. Eastlake pieces are not too graceful, but they are often sturdily constructed and made from good woods.

Most pieces are of walnut and finished with a light coat

Figure 30

A walnut Eastlake table that is
both well constructed and well designed. Current price: $100–$200.

of varnish or shellac that is easily stripped if necessary.
But one word of caution: Many of the better Eastlake-
style pieces—chairs in particular—will have backs or
posts accented with areas of walnut- or elm-burl veneers.
If they are not stripped carefully by hand, the veneers will
almost invariably come loose.

As the Eastlake style increased in popularity, manufacturers of very cheap furniture got on the bandwagon, and
so today you often find flimsily constructed headboards,
tables, and wardrobes made of very inexpensive, thin-
sawn woods such as chestnut, elm, or red oak. A typical

Figure 31

A cheaply constructed Eastlake head- and footboard in chestnut. Current price: $75–$150.

headboard of this type is only a quarter inch thick, and stripping it by any method other than by hand will cause it to warp and splinter (figure 31). Although some of this furniture does retain the typical Eastlake ornamentation, it is of hardly better quality than orange crates and should be avoided.

As the Eastlake style waned, Americans cast about for a style of home furnishings on which to anchor their still relatively undeveloped taste. World's fairs and expositions proliferated, affording the public the opportunity to see, and be swayed by, designs from all over the globe. But in spite of the excitement generated by these fairs, confusion over what was "correct" seemed to reign. Functionalism in the form of Mission wrestled with extravagance in the form of Art Nouveau, and sometimes their blood commingled. Golden Oak refereed the match, keeping score by unashamedly borrowing whatever seemed appropriate from those two styles and from any other styles its manufacturers could dream up to keep their factories smoking and the public—from rich to poor —buying. As one Grand Rapids manufacturer confidently boasted in the 1890s: "We Can Furnish the Home of the Mechanic or the Millionaire."

But every observer of the turn-of-the-century scene did not share that confidence. A writer in the *The Upholsterer* magazine could just as easily bewail the ignorance of his colleagues in the furniture trade, pointing out that

World's fairs have a tendency to educate—be it the man who fashions plowshares or the man who paints ceilings. . . . When we, in 1876, at Philadelphia, invited the world to exhibit her wares, we established what might be termed the American Renaissance. It marked the exodus of the horse-hair sofa and the advent of things Oriental. It preceded but a few years a general interest in all decorative matters.

We can recall within our own limited experience the dense ignorance of the trade no further back than 1879; the man who at that time had the courage to admire an Oriental rug was looked upon with more or less distrust as a fellow of abnormal taste. . . .

Any man who presumed to know anything of the Gothic or Renaissance was regarded as a maudlin dude. The exhibition at Paris in 1889, and at Chicago in 1893, and the exposition of this year [Paris, 1900], have proved of still greater educational value.

But the pity of it all is that the trade, which needs the education, seldom profits by the opportunities thrust upon it. It is the public—the vast purchasing public—that visits the exposition and studies the art literature. . . .

The expositions are for the studious, and the trade needs them more than the public, but the trade hasn't the time to visit them, more's the pity.

In short, it was a time of the most astonishing variety of home furnishings that Americans had ever seen and are ever likely to see again, as you yourself will discover in the next three chapters.

7

CHUNKY CHARM
THE MISSION STYLE, 1886–1930

WHAT IS NOW KNOWN in America as the Mission style had its roots in England with the Arts and Crafts Movement, whose principal proponents were two people I've already mentioned: John Ruskin and William Morris. In his own way, each advocated a return to a time of handcraftsmanship—a production of one-of-a-kind creations that recaptured the spirit of the Middle Ages, "when art and work were a form of religion."

As you may know, the American Shakers had been following those principles since about 1790, creating furniture that one author has dubbed "religion in wood." But in the late nineteenth century a man named Gustav Stickley, greatly influenced by the English Arts and Crafts Movement, combined the craftsmanship and the philosophy in ways no one had ever thought of before, producing a furniture so simple in design yet so distinctive that it was truly revolutionary.

The Historical Background

Gustav Stickley was a stonemason by training and a furniture manufacturer by choice. Apparently he first began producing handmade furniture in 1886. By 1898 he had visited England to get a firsthand look at the products inspired by the Arts and Crafts Movement and had established his Craftsman Workshops in Eastwood, New York (near Syracuse). There, he and his artisans turned out not only furniture but other forms of decorative art, including metalware. In 1901 Stickley began publishing *The Craftsman* magazine, which became, according to Robert Judson Clark in his book *The Arts and Crafts Movement in America*, "the chief spokesman for a generation of designers who established a severe, geometrical style of furniture and ornament."

Oak was Stickley's choice of wood for his furniture creations. As he himself put it in 1909, writing in *The Craftsman:*

When I first began to use the severely plain, structural forms, I chose oak as the wood that, above all others, was adapted to massive simplicity of construction. The strong, straight lines and plain surfaces of the furniture follow and emphasize the grain and growth of the wood, drawing attention to, instead of destroying, the natural character that belonged to the growing tree.

Stickley made much of his furniture by hand, using pinned mortise-and-tenon joints at critical points. But like William Morris in England, he did not disdain the use of modern machinery, asserting that "the machine can be put to all its legitimate uses as an aid to, and a preparation for, the work of the hand. . . . The machine must always *serve* man and not dehumanize him."

In addition to furniture, Stickley also designed "wholesome" bungalows that he called "Craftsman homes." These were the forerunners of the ranch-style homes of today and were always simple and functional with a great deal of wood trim. There were beams and girders, recessed window seats, and high wainscoting. Much of the furniture was designed to blend in with the wood trim, a practice that Frank Lloyd Wright later adapted by actually building furniture into the architectural design.

An interesting feature of Craftsman furniture was that its straightforward designs could be imitated by the novice furniture maker. In fact, the do-it-yourself aspect of the Arts and Crafts Movement in America was sufficiently important that *The Craftsman* magazine often featured manuals showing how to make one's own furnishings using everything from orange crates to oak boards. As Stickley himself put it, "the true American likes to know how things are done. His interest and sympathy are immediately aroused when he sees something that he really

Figure 32

A Mission chair totally constructed with pinned mortise-and-tenon joints. The style is pure
Stickley, and the chair has been
attributed to him. Current price:
$100–$200.

likes and knows to be a good thing, if he is able to feel
that if he wanted it and had the time, he could make one
like it himself." And this, I am sure, accounts for the
seemingly homemade pieces of Mission-style furniture
that occasionally crop up at flea markets.

Actually, Stickley's greatest influence was less in the
handcrafted approach to furniture than in the idea that
furnishings should be used in practical ways rather than
as decoration. He was perhaps the first American furniture designer to express in his work the concept that form
follows function, that "less is more." He was, in that
sense, ahead of his time, and it wasn't until two decades
later that his basic idea became the formal principle for

Figure 33

A Mission bookshelf of good, "honest" construction. The tenons extend through the mortises in the sides of the piece and are held in place by "key" wedges. Current price: $75–$125.

the highly influential modern designs of the Bauhaus in Weimar, Germany.

Although Stickley was the first to promote the Arts and Crafts Movement in America, he was not the most astute in terms of public relations. That honor belongs to a flamboyant character named Elbert Hubbard, or "Fra Elbertus," as he liked to call himself. A former soap salesman, Harvard dropout, and failed novelist, Hubbard established his own community of artisans in East Aurora, New York—the Roycroft Shops—where the Roycrofters made "Craft-Style" furniture and metalware.

Hubbard was a shrewd publicist, a prolific writer, a long-winded lecturer, and, for some, a spellbinding con-

Figure 34

A Mission bookcase. The leaded,
stained-glass inserts in the upper
part of the doors are very attractive and probably derived from
designs by Will H. Bradley that
appeared in the *Ladies' Home Journal*
in 1902. Current price: $200–$350.

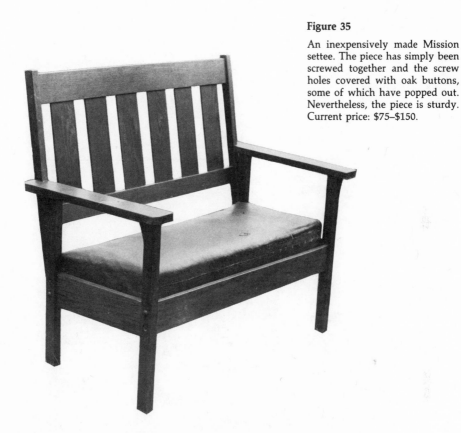

Figure 35

An inexpensively made Mission settee. The piece has simply been screwed together and the screw holes covered with oak buttons, some of which have popped out. Nevertheless, the piece is sturdy. Current price: $75–$150.

versationalist. Disciples came from miles around to listen to the words of the master as he held court at the Roycroft Inn in East Aurora. Hubbard's message, verbal and written, was always morally and spiritually uplifting. His piousness, however, didn't always find its way into his personal life, and a marital scandal in which he was the central figure left him with a fairly shabby reputation in East Aurora. But outside his home base he was looked upon as something of a prophet, and his best-known essay, "A Message to Garcia," a virtuous and inaccurate account of an incident in the Spanish-American War, is reputed to have sold eighty million copies.

In spite of the fact that both Stickley and Hubbard were espousing essentially the same philosophy, there was little love lost between them, each calling the other a "fake." Strangely enough, their careers both ended in 1915—the year that Stickley went bankrupt from overexpansion and Hubbard died on the ill-fated *Lusitania.*

The person responsible for giving Mission furniture the

Figure 36

An advertisement for a solid-oak
Mission library suite from a 1931
mail-order catalog. The original
price for all six pieces: $33.50.
Current prices: chairs, $75–$150;
desk, $125–$225; wastebasket, $15
–$30; plant stand, $25–$50.

name we know it by today was Henry L. Wilson. A Chicago builder-promoter, Wilson designed his own version of Stickley's bungalows, explaining that *his* homes displayed Oriental and Spanish colonial influences. He called it the "Mission Style," and the name stuck to the furniture as well.

As you might expect, once the Arts and Crafts fashion was underway, other manufacturers decided to get in on the act. Those who mass-produced Mission in Grand Rapids included Stickley's own brothers, who called their creations "Quaint" furniture. Turn-of-the-century Sears, Roebuck catalogs and others abounded with Mission furniture, Sears claiming somewhat disingenuously that it derived its name from the "original pieces found in an old Spanish mission in Southern California."

"Cottage furniture" was another name applied to the Arts and Crafts-inspired designs. While Mission was advertised for the masses in mail-order catalogs as well as in the more elite publications, tasteful ads for Cottage appeared only in the likes of *House Beautiful* and *House & Garden*. The look, however, was essentially the same except that Cottage pieces were slimmer than the usually chunky Mission. Much basically Mission-style furniture was also made with Art Nouveau motifs (Chapter 8).

In any case, the style was so popular that in mail-order catalogs from as late as the 1930s suites of solid-oak Mission furniture were still prominently advertised.

The Current Market

Whatever the name, oak is the wood. Of course, not all oak is of equal quality, since the mass producers were less selective in choosing wood than were the better manufacturers. Nonetheless, because of the simple designs, it was almost impossible to make Mission pieces badly, so there is a vast amount of well-made furniture available for those of you who love not only oak but a geometrical look in your furnishings.

Figure 37

A signed Stickley Morris chair with its original leather cushions. Current price: $200–$400.

Mission construction, like authentic Eastlake construction, is based on the house and furniture construction of earlier times. Basically, it is made from posts and supporting beams, comparable to the structure of old barns. All the structural parts that support weight and stress—the arms, legs, and stretchers of chairs, for example—are solid, stocky pieces of oak, thick enough so that they can be connected with mortise-and-tenon joints, a much better method than simply doweling the parts together. Sideboards and chests are similarly made, and the panels that are set into them are generally of solid oak rather than veneer. Particularly well made are the pieces that were designed for schoolrooms, libraries, offices, and waiting rooms. Even the Mission furniture in which shortcuts were taken—in which screws rather than pegs were used for joining—will be found in good condition simply because oak is such a strong wood and holds screws so well (figure 35). On some pieces you may find loose joints, but this will be the result of glue deterioration and not of a

Figure 38

Three Mission makers' trademarks found on their signed furniture. *Left to right:* Stickley; Hubbard; Rohlfs.

structural weakness in the furniture. Mission furniture can easily be reglued.

The style was to darken the wood either by fuming, staining, or applying a dark varnish. Since fuming is achieved by changing the color of the wood chemically, neither stripping nor bleaching will remove the dark color. The stained pieces, particularly the varnished ones, will look fresh and bright when stripped, however.

If you're looking for original, labeled Mission furniture, you may have some luck. Gustav Stickley used labels or stamped his furniture in inconspicuous places with a drawing of a joiner's compass and the words "Als ik kan/ Gustav Stickley." Elbert Hubbard's Roycrofters had their logo, as well, as did another New York State maker, Charles Rohlfs. However, you should be aware of the fact that there is currently a minor boom going on in the Mission market, especially where signed pieces by well-known makers are concerned. Some of the better pieces have brought thousands of dollars at auction from collectors and dealers. Even unsigned, minor pieces, such as chairs, which can be attributed to Stickley or another maker, may cost well over a hundred dollars. The point is that the market for Mission is ripe for collectors and for making financially rewarding discoveries.

8

FLOWERING FANTASIES:
ART NOUVEAU,
1893–1930

FOR THE MISSION STYLE, designers had mined the past for inspiration. But in doing so they discovered a distinctly American, and in many ways quite modern, vein of furniture. Mission broke the rules by championing a rational, studied, less-is-more unsophistication in furniture design.

Art Nouveau, on the other hand, was nothing if not a conscious effort to break with the past and create a totally modern idiom. As far as the designers of much Art Nouveau furniture were concerned, more was often more—in floral ornamentation, curvilinear shapes, and, what was altogether new, an occasional foray into the world of asymmetricality. Though far from actually breaking with the past—much Art Nouveau seems to be patently derived from Louis XV designs—Art Nouveau did effectively divorce itself from the commonplace. The style not only aspired to supersophistication but also to an overall effect that could easily strike the observer, perhaps only on a subconscious level, as slightly naughty, decadent, and dangerous. A room filled with fully developed French Art Nouveau furniture—carved with writhing, feral, organic forms—could just as easily be found in the haze of an opium-induced hallucination as in the clear light of the real world.

But I'm speaking here as though *Art Nouveau* were an all-encompassing term for a coherent style, which it is not.

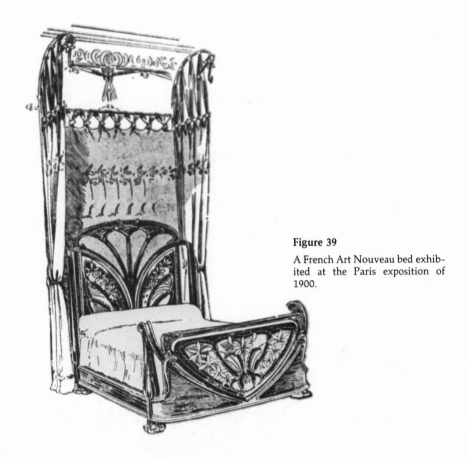

Figure 39

A French Art Nouveau bed exhibited at the Paris exposition of 1900.

Art Nouveau furniture was produced by many different Western industrialized countries, and each had a different name for the style—for instance, Métro Style, Inglese Style, Sezessionstil, Yachting Style, Modernismo, Jugendstil, and Glasgow School. In fact, there were two different, basic schools of Art Nouveau. The best known is the Franco-Belgian, which could range from relatively subdued sophistication to flowering fantasies. The other school, that of Glasgow and Vienna, produced quite simple, rectilinear furniture, which was often inlaid or otherwise decorated with organic shapes, portraits of young women smelling flowers, and the like. The latter style was more akin to Arts and Crafts Movement designs than anything else. The term *Art Nouveau* (or, more accurately, *L'Art Nouveau*), which the style ultimately came to be called in America, was derived from the name of the shop

The Historical Background

Figure 40

Top: detail of the crest-rail carving.
Bottom: a set of six oak American
Art Nouveau chairs showing the
influence of the Vienna school.
Current price, the set: $200–$400.

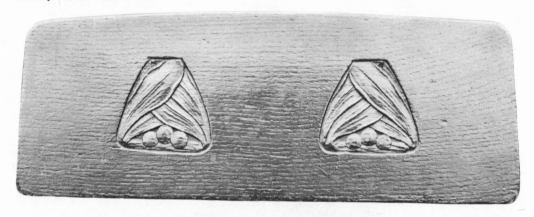

Figure 41

An American Art Nouveau armchair in its pure form, French-inspired and manufactured in 1901
by the Grand Rapids firm of Ret-
ting and Sweet. Current price: $75
–$175. (*The Grand Rapids Furniture
Record*, 1901)

of French oriental art dealer Samuel Bing. His Salon de
L'Art Nouveau, which he opened in Paris in 1895, fea-
tured, among other objects, glassware by one Louis C.
Tiffany.

After its official introduction at the Paris exposition of
1889 (for which, incidentally, the Eiffel Tower was constructed), Art Nouveau's first inroads into American design were seen at the World's Columbian Exposition, held
in Chicago in 1893. There the Grand Rapids Chair Company exhibited what has come to be called a side-by-side

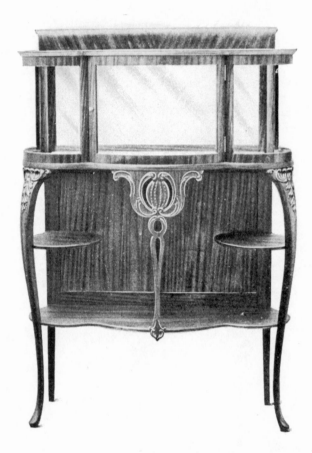

Figure 42

The American conception of Art Nouveau: a mahogany server made by the Berkey Furniture Company, Grand Rapids. Current price: $200–$400. (*The Grand Rapids Furniture Record,* 1901; see also figure 97)

—a type of desk-bookcase whose asymmetricality echoes elements of certain French Art Nouveau designs. By the early 1900s Art Nouveau, in one form or another, was being mass produced in America at a fairly good clip.

Which brings up an interesting question. Perhaps parroting each other, many authorities in the past have asserted that Art Nouveau had very little influence on American furniture design. But is this the case? I don't think so. The problem, I think, is that many people don't recognize American Art Nouveau furniture when they see it; but the more you look, the more you see it.

The fact is that Art Nouveau fascinated, mystified, and frightened American furniture manufacturers. In 1900 *The*

Upholsterer magazine could inform its readers that "the Paris Exposition of 1900 has done at least one thing—it has introduced L'Art Nouveau and left its indellible [sic] impression upon all interested in things decorative." Soon afterward *The Grand Rapids Furniture Record* was showing illustrations of American Art Nouveau pieces from the Grand Rapids Spring Exhibition and Sale, optimistically commenting that the "new departure in L'Art Nouveau excited considerable interest," but adding morosely:

> The manufacturers are going somewhat slow in this direction, however, and the retailers do not seem to embrace the innovation enthusiastically. Perhaps the consumer will, when he has a chance to compare the unique style with the elaborate ornate [i.e., Golden Oak], which at present seems to enjoy the most popularity.

However, the *Record* came closer to the truth when it pointed out on another page that

> L'Art Nouveau is exemplified in several mahogany suites, and this [American] conception of the new art is in decided contrast to a good deal of the designs put out under the French name. To the mind of the RECORD man it is the conception that is likely to prove popular and effective in this country.

The Current Market

All this is not to say that you will not find Art Nouveau in its relatively pure form, produced by American manufacturers. You will, if you look hard enough. But, as usual, most American manufacturers adapted Art Nouveau to their own needs, borrowing whatever elements they felt were right for the market and would sell. Thus the American Art Nouveau furniture you'll find will more often than not have distinctly Art Nouveau motifs, such as tapering supports for display shelves, tulip carvings or cutouts, or simply carved, curvilinear organic designs. Furthermore, although they may at first seem like strange bedfellows, Mission and Art Nouveau got along quite well. That shouldn't be too surprising in light of the fact that the Glasgow and Vienna products were themselves inspired by the Arts and Crafts Movement. As a result,

Figure 43

In Grand Rapids, Gustav Stickley's brothers mass-produced Art Nouveau furniture with Arts and Crafts touches. Current prices: $75–$175. (*The Grand Rapids Furniture Record,* 1901)

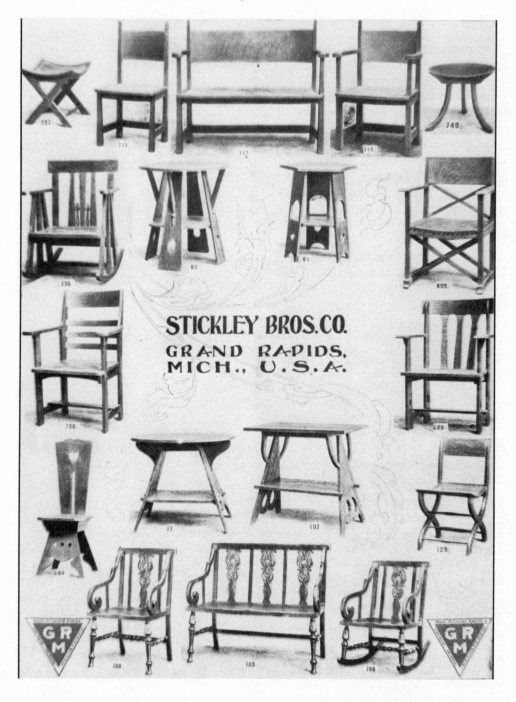

Figure 44

An oak Art Nouveau table decorated with shallow carving. Current price: $100–$225.

you'll find basic, oak Mission furniture with floral carvings, inlays, marquetry, or cutouts, and often with reverse-tapering legs (wider at the bottom than at the top)—all a concession to the influence of Art Nouveau. Indeed, obvious Art Nouveau motifs can be found on mass-produced furniture well into the 1930s, and so perhaps those who downplay the style's influence should revise their opinions.

But I'm not trying to start an argument here. My real point is that you, the used-furniture buyer, should not overlook Art Nouveau just because others are overlooking it. One good reason for this is that currently, since it does go unrecognized by many buyers and dealers, Art Nouveau is very reasonably priced. Another reason is that with a little effort almost anyone could put together a good collection of American Art Nouveau in a variety of interesting woods including weathered oak and nicely figured mahogany. Finally, it is as well made as any other style of mass-produced furniture.

So keep your eyes open for American Art Nouveau. I don't think you'll be disappointed.

Figure 45

Note the pressed Art Nouveau pattern in the crest rail of this oak rocking chair advertised in a 1931 mail-order catalog. Current price: $125–$175.

Figure 46

Inspired by the Vienna School and designed by John Brower, this bedroom suite in solid gumwood, stained green, was manufactured by the Sligh Furniture Company, Grand Rapids, in 1907. Its simplicity and rounded edges anticipated by more than a quarter century the Depression Modern designs of the 1930s. Estimated current price, the four-piece suite including a chair (not shown): $1,000–$1,500.

Figure 47

The "McKinley Chair" and the "McKinley Rocker," first produced in 1896 and subsequently patented by the Phoenix Furniture Company of Grand Rapids; so named because photos of presidential candidate McKinley's Ohio home showed the chair. The chair is oak, the rocker bent mahogany plywood. Are these pieces Art Nouveau, or Mission, or just curiously modern? I'll let you decide. Current price: $125–$175. (*The Grand Rapids Furniture Record,* 1901)

9

"ELABORATE ORNATE":
GOLDEN OAK, 1890–1930

SINCE THE 1960s, many of you have been filling your homes with oak furniture, vintage about 1890 to 1930. Perhaps you bought it because it was inexpensive, and as the years have gone by you've probably been amazed and delighted to discover that your bargains of yesterday are the "new antiques" of today. Even more pleasant is the fact that these pieces have doubled and tripled in value.

Who would have thought that these machine-made, often mail-order pieces would become collector's items? Certainly not their original purchasers. They bought them for the same reason you did—because they were the best buys in town.

The Historical Background

Golden Oak is not so much a style of furniture as it is a type, one that can usually (but not always) best be described as *The Grand Rapids Furniture Record* did in the article quoted in the previous chapter: "elaborate ornate." Its name in this country is derived from its usually honey-colored finish, but the furniture originated in England, where it was called Edwardian. Somehow Edwardian furniture was never able to climb from downstairs to upstairs in its homeland, but in America it was enthusiastically embraced. Indeed, it became the most popular furniture this country has ever produced, or is ever likely to in the future.

To a country accustomed to many decades of Victorian furniture, the stark functionalism of Mission must have been a bit hard to take for some of the populace. But in

Figure 48

A bedroom furnished with Bassett
Furniture Industries Golden Oak
made about 1910. Current price,
matching three-piece bedroom
suite: $700–$1,200.

Golden Oak the public found a fashion that uniquely
reflected the needs and yearnings of the late nineteenth
century. There was plenty of ornamentation and carving
—as much as you wanted to pay for, in fact—which made
the furniture familiar looking, and it had a sufficiently
European feel to make it fashionable. The light-colored
oak was less formal than the dark Victorian, and the
smaller scale of the furniture made it suitable for urban
living. In addition, although the pieces could be graceful
in design, they were also extremely sturdy and didn't
have to be relegated to the front parlor to be gingerly sat
upon only by Sunday company.

The oak these pieces were made of was in terrific abun-
dance and was, therefore, cheap. Besides, the manufacturers didn't have to use the finest oak: Those turned
spindle-backs and legs and stretchers of chairs were very

Figure 49

An extraordinarily elaborate Golden Oak rocking chair made by the Michigan Chair Company, Grand Rapids. Current price: $175 –$275. (*The Grand Rapids Furniture Record,* 1900)

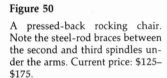

Figure 50

A pressed-back rocking chair. Note the steel-rod braces between the second and third spindles under the arms. Current price: $125–$175.

easily made with less-than-prime woods. Another plus for Golden Oak was that it was perfectly suited for the new technology that had almost reached present-day levels of sophistication. Power machinery could mass-produce even the most intricate and delicate designs, while skilled labor was needed only to set up the machines, not to actually operate them.

Last but not least, the burgeoning immigrant popula-
tion provided a cheap labor market and, in turn, a market
for cheap consumer goods, while new merchandising
methods in the form of mail-order houses were able to
supply this market. The mail-order houses not only elimi-
nated the middle man, thus enabling them to sell less
expensively—it's hard to beat a ninety-eight-cent chair—
but they offered ironclad guarantees as well and were
more than willing to sell on credit. Buying on credit was,
of course, not without its hazards. *The Grand Rapids Furniture Record* reported one case in which a poor Indiana wom-
an had begun a lawsuit against a furniture company for

> so cursing and frightening her as to make her sick.
> She purchased on the installment plan; and, while
> she was confined to her bed with three-days-old
> infant, the collector, enraged at being unable to make
> collection, cursed and threatened her and called her
> a liar. She asks for $5,000 damages.

In any case, all the aforementioned factors contributed
to making Golden Oak the people's furniture, yet with
enough variety of design so that everyone's home could
look just a bit different. At the turn of the century, for
example, just one manufacturer in Grand Rapids advertised that it produced over twenty-five hundred designs
in twenty-five different furniture forms, and that was by
no means unusual.

There was never any pretense that Golden Oak was
handmade. On the contrary, pieces were proudly iden-
tified as products of Grand Rapids, and top designers
came from Europe to create original and sophisticated
designs that were then churned out by the factories. In
fact, mass-produced furnishings were in such demand
that dozens of small towns set up their own factories to
produce oak pieces in imitation of the big-city manufacturers. The ornamentation came from itinerant carvers,
whose peculiarly personal carving patterns were sometimes quite beautiful, other times fairly bizarre; but those
decorations made many of the pieces appear to be one-of-
a-kind productions. The goal, however, was not only to
be different but to have a prestigious factory label. There-

Figure 51

The Welsh Folding Bed Company of Grand Rapids specialized in its namesake. The fronts of these pieces fold down to form the bed. The ad illustrates only a small sampling of the company's entire line. Current price: $300–$450. (*The Grand Rapids Furniture Record*, 1900)

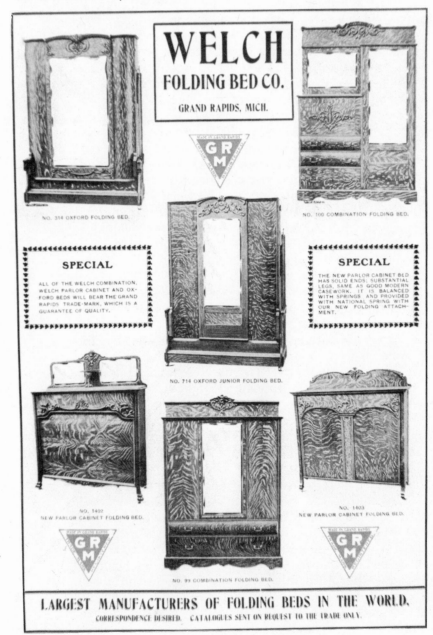

Figure 52

The Karges Furniture Company of Evansville, Indiana, competed with Grand Rapids manufacturers on even terms, as these designs from a 1900 Karges catalog demonstrate. Current price: $150–$300.

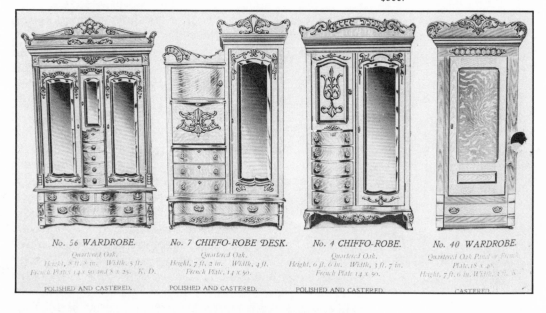

No. 56 WARDROBE.
Quartered Oak.
Height, 8 ft. 8 in.   Width, 5 ft.
French Plates 14 x 50 and 8 x 25.   K. D.
POLISHED AND CASTERED.

No. 7 CHIFFO-ROBE DESK.
Quartered Oak.
Height, 7 ft. 2 in.   Width, 4 ft.
French Plate, 14 x 50.
POLISHED AND CASTERED.

No. 4 CHIFFO-ROBE.
Quartered Oak.
Height, 6 ft. 6 in.   Width, 3 ft. 7 in.
French Plate 14 x 50.
POLISHED AND CASTERED.

No. 40 WARDROBE.
Quartered Oak Panel or French
Plate, 18 x 48.
Height, 7 ft. 6 in.   Width, 3 ft. 8 in.
CASTERED.

Figure 53

A good Golden Oak sideboard. Current price: $300–$400.

fore some of the smaller manufacturers saw fit to incorporate "Grand Rapids" into their company names and furniture labels—a practice that was later stopped by the Federal Trade Commission.

All in all it was an exciting period of expansion in the furniture industry. In 1908, at the semiannual market held at Grand Rapids, more than two hundred firms exhibited their wares. In the next few years the number of exhibitors more than tripled.

As Golden Oak aficionados know quite well, what makes this mass-produced furniture so appealing is its tremendous variety. The furniture designers borrowed from, and brazenly combined, elements from every period imaginable. Carved lion's feet were stolen from French Empire furniture (by way of Egypt); Art Nouveau designs were stamped into pressed-back chairs that otherwise resembled American Federal furniture of the early nineteenth century. If you wished, you could buy a "Napoleon bed" just like the one slept in by Napoleon I; or you could have more simple "Colonial" furniture, which in reality was a variation of American Empire scroll-foot furniture originally popular not during the Colonial period at all but during the 1830–40 period. Some chairs did hark back to Colonial times, while others incorporated wood-bending techniques employed in making snowshoes and toboggans or borrowed from European bentwood furniture. In short, there seemed to be something for everyone, and everyone for something.

By 1920 Golden Oak was at its resplendent gaudiest, plastered with such massive quantities of ornament that the underlying furniture threatened to disappear. But by the end of the twenties the trend had abated considerably, and the oak furniture shown in mail-order catalogs is of simpler design or imitative of English styles.

The Current Market

Golden Oak furniture was made for offices, public buildings, and factories as well as for the home. So, when canvassing the used-furniture market, you'll discover a variety of useful, handsome pieces, including: kitchen cupboards, chests of drawers, and headboards (some incised with carving for a pseudo-Jacobean look); secretary-

Figure 54

The Nelson-Matter Furniture Company's "Napoleon" bed (*center*) was a popular but comparatively simple design. Current prices, individual pieces: $150–$200. (*The Grand Rapids Furniture Record,* 1901)

Figure 55

A dark-stained maple rocking chair with the mass-producer's idea of the 1740–60 Queen Anne style in the shape of the splat and in the crest-rail carving. Current price: $125–$175.

Figure 56

By the early 1930s, mail-order Golden Oak furniture had become quite simplified. Current price: $250–$450.

Figure 57

Left: Hoosier Cabinet is the generic term for all kitchen cupboards like this one. This particular piece was manufactured by the Sellers Company of Indiana; each of the door latches is embossed with an *S*. The tall left-hand door conceals a built-in flour bin and sifter, the countertop slides in and out, and the lower right-hand drawer is a metal-lined bread box. In the earliest such cupboards, the countertops are zinc; this one, from about 1920, is porcelain over iron. The fancier models have a tall right-hand door concealing a sugar bin. Current price: $250–$350. *Below:* a "want list" shopping dial and cookbook holder tacked into an upper door of a Hoosier Cabinet actually made by the Hoosier Cabinet Company, New Castle, Indiana. (See also figures 70 and 79.)

Figure 58

Left: a typical asymmetrical side-by-side. *Right:* a less common double side-by-side. Current prices: $250–$500.

bookcases (the so-called side-by-sides); dining tables with massive legs or with pedestal bases; graceful rockers and side chairs; elaborate library tables and straighter, simpler factory cutting tables; and rolltop office desks.

Despite the name, golden was not the only color nor oak the only wood used in Golden Oak. Some of the furniture was finished in darker tones to give it a more traditional look, although most of it was simply varnished. Thus, if necessary, Golden Oak may be easily stripped by the cold-tank process, and the wood, even if covered by a time-darkened varnish, will regain its original look. Chairs were frequently constructed of combina-

Figure 59

At the turn of the century the St. Johns Table Company was the world's largest producer of "extension, breakfast, kitchen, library, parlor, office, saloon, [and] restaurant tables." Current prices: square tables, $150–$300; round tables, $350–$550. (*The Grand Rapids Furniture Record,* 1900)

tions of two or more woods, such as ash, maple, hickory, and beech. Those woods do match well enough so that you can give them a uniform appearance after stripping. But you should carefully examine pieces other than chairs —for example, washstands, chests, and bedside tables. Some of them were made very cheaply for rooming houses, summer cottages, and small-town hotels, and their construction may be very poor. The woods may be elm, soft maple, or chestnut; the latter in particular may emerge from a stripping tank with a rough, splintery finish.

You should also be aware of the fact that Golden Oak

Figure 60

A pedestal table with exceptional carving on the legs. Current price: $600–$900.

Figure 61

A deluxe S-curve rolltop desk with a multitude of pigeonholes, probably made for an office (note the label holders on the drawers). The S-curve (i.e., double curve) in rolltops is considered better than the single curve. This particular piece is a proud product of the Valley City Desk Company, Grand Rapids. Current price: $1,000–$2,000. (*The Grand Rapids Furniture Record,* 1900)

Figure 62

The "sectional" bookcase, whose sections can be stacked or arranged side by side in various configurations, is an American invention of the Golden Oak era. Current price: $275–$375.

Figure 63

A so-called lady's rolltop with an S-curve top. Current price: $300–$400.

pieces manufactured after World War I were often veneered. Look closely at dining-table and desktops and at the sides and doors of cabinets. You're likely to find a chestnut core with a thin layer of oak veneer applied to both sides of it. Tabletops may be made of chunks of miscellaneous woods that have been assembled like a jigsaw puzzle and then veneered. In most cases, only the most careful stripping processes will preserve these pieces. Also, except on chair legs and pedestal-table bases, you'll have to check any raised carving; except on the finest pieces, you can assume that carved decorations are glued on, and after stripping you'll probably have to reglue them.

And, as I've mentioned before, please try to avoid non-factory-painted pieces—not only because you'll have no

Figure 64

The best in Golden Oak iceboxes, with applied carving and fancy brass hinges. Note the ice-water tap and glass holder on the right-hand side. Current price: $300–$400. (*The Grand Rapids Furniture Record,* 1900)

way of knowing what damage the paint may be disguising but also because it is virtually impossible to strip paint from the grain and turnings of oak and other woods. Rolltop desks have special problems: the canvas to which the strips of wood were glued to make the rolltop becomes brittle with age, and the wood strips may require remounting (see Chapter 5). Oak iceboxes, which many people are converting into bars and storage cabinets, should never be dip-stripped: the chemicals are absorbed by the insulation (usually cork or rock wool), causing the box to drip and smell.

Like the vast oak forests themselves, once upon a time

Figure 65

A far simpler oak icebox than the preceding, but still a handsome piece. Current price: $200–$300.

the supply of Golden Oak furniture seemed inexhaustible. But demand for Golden Oak has been so strong that dealers have had to turn to new sources, notably the British Isles. At first glance the European pieces look very much like the native product, and they are well constructed. But if on second glance you feel that something is missing, you're right. By and large the European pieces lack the style and exuberance of American Golden Oak; they're simply more staid, more formal.

Since Golden Oak is becoming scarce, especially in sets such as bedroom suites or even sets of six matching chairs, you may well wonder if Golden Oak will ever achieve

Figure 66

The ultimate in Golden Oak Morris chairs, from a turn-of-the-century mail-order catalog. As the ad points out, "the back of this chair is adjustable to four different reclining positions by means of a ratchet attachment." Current price: $175–$275.

values comparable to those of true antiques. The fact is that some Golden Oak already costs *more* than certain pieces of handmade, antique American furniture that is a hundred years older! Golden Oak is even being reproduced with fairly good fidelity—always a good indication that demand is threatening to outstrip supply. A table that only a few years ago cost sixty dollars may now cost three hundred, and no doubt it will soon fetch nine hundred. The point is that, if you favor Golden Oak, the time to buy is now.

10

HODGEPODGE LODGES:
THE BARONIAL STYLE OF THE 1920s

WITH THE ONSET of World War I, innovation in the American furniture industry came to a halt and remained fairly stagnant during the immediate postwar years. For a while the middle class contented itself with Golden Oak and Mission, while the affluent minority decorated in English and French period styles. In much of America it was also a time of what has been called the "period house."

The Historical Background

The wealthy were literally building their castles. The middle class were moving to that new area called the suburbs—formerly farmland around cities, of course—and they wanted their castles, too, or at least "castlettes." So the architects obliged, basing their designs on their personal interpretations of Spanish or Colonial or Norman or Breton styles. But by and large the most popular style seems to have been "Tudor," with its mock half-timbering and hodgepodge of Jacobean, Gothic, and Romanesque motifs.

If you couldn't afford antiques for your period house—even the brand-new "antiques" being produced in Europe—you still needed appropriate furniture, and the Baronial styles filled the bill nicely.

By about 1924 these Castle or Baronial styles of furniture were being mass-produced in this country in suites, and much of the manufacturing was being done in the South, which was quickly eclipsing Grand Rapids as the furniture capital of America. Unlike the European manu-

Figure 67

A 1920s dining room furnished in the Baronial style with pieces made by Bassett Furniture Industries. Current prices: set of four side chairs, $100–$250; gate leg table, $100–$200; sideboard, $150–$200.

facturers, the Americans did not try to simulate antiques through elaborate shading of the finish or distressing to create the illusion of age, nor were the finishes referred to as Ye Olde English Brown or Aged Tudor. And furniture advertisements rarely dared to claim that the Baronial styles were true reproductions of Gothic or Italian Renaissance furniture. However, they would go so far as to maintain that the furniture was "massively designed in Gothic period style, with finish and decoration typical of 15th and 16th century English furniture. Rich in design and detail." If there was anything that could vaguely be called innovation, it could be seen in the solid-front china cabinet ("much more fashionable than the old-style cabinets with glass doors!") or in the "Fashionable Refectory Table: Extension leaves at each end fit under the top.

Figure 68

American walnut bedroom furniture in the "Italian Renaissance Style" from a 1922 Karges Furniture Company catalog. Current prices: bed, $150–$250; chiffonier, $100–$175; chest of drawers (dresser), $100–$200, nightstand, $30–$50; bench, $40–$60; chair, $40–$60.

When you pull them out, they rise automatically and lock into position."

Suites of inexpensive Baronial furniture were known in the trade as "borax," which Martin Greif has called:

a wonderful American term that has all but vanished from the language. Because hawkers of the then-famous cleanser, Twenty Mule Team Borax, had of-

Figure 69

The Baronial style persisted into the 1930s. This "borax" bedroom suite was advertised in a 1932 mail-order catalog. Current price, three-piece suite: $400–$600.

fered as free premiums cheap and garish kitsch, the word "borax" came to be associated with the "extra" values offered by commercial furniture manufacturers: "extra" carving, "extra" large-size frames, "extra" glossy finish.

One wonders if the manufacturers' apparent contempt for their own borax merely masked their chagrin at foisting the stuff on the public in the first place.

If the 1920s were something of a low point in American furniture design, there were nonetheless a few notable things going on. The reproductions and adaptations of eighteenth-century English and French provincial styles that began to resurface led to a mode of decoration that we more or less take for granted today, namely, furnish-

Figure 70

This model of Hoosier Cabinet
was available in green, gray, or
white enamel inside and out, or in
a Golden Oak exterior finish with
a green enamel interior, according
to the ad in a 1931 mail-order
catalog. Current prices: painted
exterior, $175–$275; Golden Oak
exterior, $225–$325.

Figure 71

A Baronial breakfast suite advertised in a 1931 mail-order catalog. Current price, the suite: $175–$275.

ing different rooms in different furniture styles. More important, the changing pattern in housing and mass-production technology brought with them everything from mechanical refrigerators to electric sewing machines, sophisticated radios to forms of furniture that were previously unknown.

For the first time kitchens were designed with an eye to function and appearance. Coal, wood, and kerosene ranges gave way to gas and electric ones. Refrigerators, stoves, and sinks were enameled, usually in off-white or pale blue, yellow, or green, so that all the appliances matched. And the eat-in kitchen was born when a space was set aside for "breakfast room" suites of tables and chairs, painted to match the appliances. Enameled sinks replaced those of zinc or stoneware, and kitchens were painted in brighter colors. Built-in cabinets and linoleum-covered counters began to appear.

Outside of the kitchen a new piece of furniture cropped up in the living room: the coffee table. And for the first time the public was offered suites of scaled-down furniture for the children's room.

The Current Market

More often than not, case pieces of Baronial furniture were proudly proclaimed as being constructed of native gumwood, and there was even a gumwood association that publicized the merits of their namesake. Just why, however, is something of a mystery. Other than having a bland, close grain and a color in the raw that ranges from parsnip to purplish green—all characteristics that make it easy to stain—gum has no merits as a furniture wood that makes it worth crowing about. Furthermore, what was not advertised as being made from gum was frankly described as only veneered with "genuine" walnut, oak, or what have you.

In spite of that the Baronial styles seem to be the most sought-after used furniture after Golden Oak. Because it is massive and seems to be solid and well made, because it has such earmarks of bygone craftsmanship as carvings, turnings, and elaborate veneers, and because it may look older than it is, many uninformed buyers are drawn to it. But I'm here to tell you that, if it's necessary, Baronial furniture is by far the most difficult to strip and refinish.

Most Baronial furniture has all the drawbacks I've warned you about in previous chapters on quality. The turnings and carvings are glued up from small pieces with synthetic glues, and so are the veneers. The stained gumwood looks lifeless and dull gray after stripping, and it generally requires restaining rather than simple varnishing.

On the whole, Baronial furniture of the twenties and early thirties should be purchased with the utmost caution. As Golden Oak becomes rarer and hence more expensive, the Baronial styles will be more in demand. But

Figure 72

A well-made Baronial chair manufactured by the Gunlocke Company, Wayland, New York. It's made of solid, not glued-up, hardwood, and the carving is finely detailed. The tapestry look of the upholstery is typical of this furniture. Current price: $100–$175.

unless you can use it as it is, or revive it, it is rarely worth refinishing.

Regarding breakfast-room furniture: As well as being factory-painted to match the appliances, it was also sold unfinished, ready to be painted and decorated by the buyer (another twenties innovation). But whether factory- or buyer-painted, you are unlikely to find good wood beneath the layers of paint. For example, hardwood tops, often of gum, and fir bases were the usual woods used in kitchen tables.

In 1925 the government of France, being somewhat apprehensive about the ascendancy of other countries in the industrial arts, sponsored in Paris one of the most famous international expositions ever held. Most countries were represented, but America was conspicuous by her absence. Writing five years later in 1930, American designer Paul Frankl explained that the only reason America was not represented . . . was that we found we had no decorative art. Not only was there a sad lack of achievement that could be exhibited, but we discovered that there was not even a serious movement in this direction and that the general public was quite unconscious that modern art had been extended into the field of business and industry.

But ten years after the Paris exposition Americans were buying and living with perhaps the most remarkable and novel home furnishings that this or any other country had ever produced. How this happened, and why, is the subject of the next chapter.

11

CLEAN MACHINE:
DEPRESSION MODERN AND OTHER STYLES OF THE 1930s

WHILE AMERICA WAS NAPPING—as far as furniture design was concerned—Europe, if not exactly doing calisthenics, at least had her eyes open.

In Germany the Bauhaus school, led by such lights as Walter Gropius, Ludwig Miës van der Rohe, Marcel Breuer, and László Moholy-Nagy, was experimenting with innovative designs in furniture, architecture, typography, and weaving, among other crafts. Although many of the Bauhaus designs are today synonymous with what we generally think of as a quintessentially contemporary, international style, the school had little influence outside of Germany in the twenties. In Scandinavia furniture design was taking a different modern tack; it, too, would later anchor itself in our consciousness, seemingly permanently.

But in the 1920s it was once again the French who took a final stab at setting the standard for international taste in the decorative arts with their new style, Art Deco.

The Historical Background

Although you'll hear "Art Deco" used as a blanket term to cover any sort of furniture that smacks of the thirties, that's far from what it is or was. The term, in English, is derived from the official title of the Paris exposition of 1925—*L'Exposition Internationale des Arts Décoratifs et Industriels Modernes.* The furniture shown in the expo was the closest thing there has ever been in the furniture world to Parisian haute couture in the fashion world. The designers of this furniture—some of whom were the original creators of Art Nouveau—and its buyers thought of themselves as

Figure 73

A rare photograph of a fine suite of Art Deco bedroom furniture made by the John Widdicomb Company, 1925–30. Note the elaborate inlay work and the detailed carving of the simulated tassels on the tops of the legs of the desk, nightstand, and beds. Estimated current price, the suite: $2,000–$3,000.

tastemakers, part of the "smart set." Thus the furniture itself was elitist by its very nature.

Art Deco is characterized by opulence and extravagance. Only the finest leathers, lacquers, enamels, velvets, snakeskin, rosewood, Macassar ebony, ivory, and other costly materials were good enough for the style the Parisians called *L'art décoratif moderne.* And, to paraphrase Cole Porter, as far as ornament was concerned, anything went. The opening of King Tut's tomb in 1922 gave designers the green light to attach pyramids and other Egyptian motifs to the furniture. If you didn't like that, you could

Figure 74

A vanity from an American Art Deco bedroom suite. Current price: $125–$225.

have Babylonio-Mayan ziggurats, or Empire tassels (in plaster and wood), or Greco-Aztec frets and sunbursts, or borrowings from the exotic costumes of the Russian Ballet.

Now although America was not officially represented in Paris, America had representatives, who for the first time saw what one museum director has called "the eclectic 'good taste' of Swedish 'Modern' and the trivial bad taste of Paris 'modernistic.'" It was the modernistic, the Art Deco, that captivated visiting Americans. Excited by it all, American designers hastened home, hoping to interest American manufacturers in producing this newfangled furniture. But most manufacturers balked; it was simply too much, too soon.

Then, in 1927, a few of the posh New York department stores held an exhibit of the French pieces from the Paris

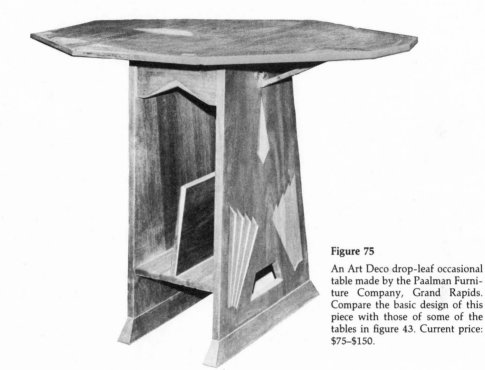

Figure 75

An Art Deco drop-leaf occasional table made by the Paalman Furniture Company, Grand Rapids. Compare the basic design of this piece with those of some of the tables in figure 43. Current price: $75–$150.

expo. There was a flurry of interest from then-prevailing tastemakers—always both attuned to the whims of the public and attempting to fine-tune those whims as well— and so the manufacturers finally decided to give the new designs a try. The result was some of the most bizarre furniture that has ever been mass-produced in America.

Pirating the ornamental motifs of Art Deco and reducing them to their lowest common denominator, the manufacturers proceeded to tack these squiggles, zigzags, and sunbursts onto furniture chassis that, if anything, resembled much earlier French designs. The pieces were "modernistic" and often imitated the designs of Hollywood sets or the architecture of the Chrysler Building or Radio City Music Hall. Few people bought the furniture, and many who did later threw it away. So today American Art Deco furniture is relatively rare. I happen to like

Figure 76

Depression Modern designs produced by the Hastings Table Company, Hastings, Michigan. Current prices: coffee tables, $75–$175; desk, $125–$225.

it because it's outrageous and makes me laugh. But many people I know don't get the joke.

Perhaps you're now asking: If there's so little American Art Deco around, then what's all the stuff the shops sell that they call Deco? Ninety-five percent of the time it's Depression Modern, the style that really predominated in the 1930s.

Despite the fact that America and the rest of the world had gotten off on the wrong foot economically, the thirties were a great period in American design. In fact, it could be argued that the thirties were the first and only period of American design—particularly the years be-

Figure 77

This Depression Modern dressing table made by the John Widdicomb Company has tiger maple veneer on the drawer fronts. Current price: $250–$450.

tween Chicago's Century of Progress Exposition (1933–34) and the New York World's Fair (1939–40). Out of this period came designs so energetic, revolutionary, and modern that their influence has been felt ever since (although it frequently goes unrecognized today).

Several factors contributed to the design revolution. The Bauhaus had already been visited by many American designers, and many of those originally associated with the school had escaped to America when the school was closed by the Nazis in 1933. These Bauhaus émigrés—the supreme proponents of functionalism in style and mass production in method—unquestionably had a hand in changing America's concept of what was modern and

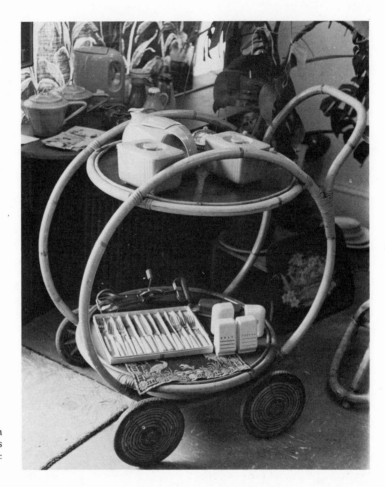

Figure 78

A Depression Modern tea cart in bamboo. Not one straight line is visible on the piece. Current price: $100–$175.

what was not. Second, America was increasingly coming to believe that science and technology were something of a new religion. As Bauhaus member and founder of the influential Chicago Institute of Design, László Moholy-Nagy, put it:

> The reality of our century is technology: the invention, construction, and maintenance of the machine.

To be a user of the machine is to be of the spirit of this century. It has replaced the transcendent spiritualism of past eras.

Nowhere did that sort of proselytizing have a greater impact, or seem to promise a brighter future, than in the most industrialized and powerful country in the world. Nowhere were people more persuaded that progress was not only possible but that it was good as well. That more than twenty-two million people attended the Chicago Century of Progress expo attests to the fact.

And so onto the American scene emerged a new breed of professional, the industrial designer, whose job it was to style objects so that they looked modern. It made no difference what the objects were—trains or teapots, planes or pencil sharpeners, automobiles or adding machines—the industrial designer streamlined them and made them look clean and sleek. Having discovered that rounding off the sharp edges of trains, planes, and cars not only allowed them to move faster but made them *look* as though they moved faster, the industrial designer could apply the same principle to any object. Thus a pencil sharpener that looked like a rocket ship was not only appealing to the eye but bespoke the latest state of the art in pencil sharpeners. And so it was with furniture.

Working with large manufacturers of mass-produced furniture—and, indeed, reacting against the modernistic jumble that was Art Deco—such designers as Raymond Loewy, Donald Deskey, Russel Wright, Kem Weber, and Gilbert Rohde created the first modern, democratic furnishings not only for the home but for offices, banks, public restrooms, nightclubs, movie theaters, and more. The style was usually rounded and always clean and functional with very little ornament except for a few (usually three) parallel lines in upholstery piping or in wood or metal moldings. Sometimes highly figured woods were used, but solid cabinet woods also began to make a comeback, including the "blonde" maple of Russel Wright's famous American Modern line. Tubular metal furniture for indoor use also appeared.

In addition to new designs, innovative approaches to

Figure 79

Right: Kitchen furniture also became streamlined during the thirties. Compare this Sellers Company Hoosier Cabinet with the one in figure 57, made about fifteen years earlier by the same company. Current price: $150–$250.

Figure 80

Below: An overstuffed Depression Modern club chair. Similar pieces can also be found with two-color upholstery, usually maroon and green. Note the three parallel lines of piping on the sides. Current price: $125–$225.

furniture could also be seen simply in the way it was marketed. For the first time the public could now buy modular furniture: matching pieces sold in individual units that could be rearranged in a variety of ways, thus suiting the personal needs of the buyer but not straining the pocketbooks of those who could not afford an entire suite of furniture. In addition, you could now buy furniture of the same coherent design, from the same line, for any and every room of the house. And, with the exception of certain large, stuffed pieces, the furniture became smaller in scale—a marketing approach intended to tantalize apartment dwellers.

But far from appealing only to "city slickers"—as Art Deco had done—Depression Modern was a style that

Figure 81

Left: A well-designed Depression Modern tubular metal chair that is both functional and comfortable. The two buttons at the base prevent the chair from tipping forward. Current price: $75–$125.

Figure 82

Below: An inexpensive and common Depression Modern end table. The mirrored top is tinted blue; similar pieces can be found with peach- and, more rarely, green-tinted tops. Current price: $30–$60.

sped across America faster than the Burlington Zephyr. From New York City to Rapid City, the public liked it and bought it. The Tulsa, Oklahoma, *Tribune* even saw fit to editorialize about the new style:

> The best furniture in the world today is made right here in the little old U.S.A. The up-to-date home is furnished with up-to-date furniture, modern in pattern, modern in workmanship. . . . Be a progressive and don't be ashamed to be a good patriot when you go to the furniture shop. Be a modernist in your furniture no less than in your literary taste or your social aspirations.

In short, the machine had finally been turned to the advantage of the decorative arts in America.

Figure 83

This vanity, produced by the John Widdicomb Company, incorporates the three parallel lines of Depression Modern furniture in the design of its top and drawer pulls. Current price: $200–$400.

Figure 84

A suite of Waterfall bedroom furniture. Pieces with this general design were manufactured from the late 1930s through the early 1950s. *Waterfall* refers to the V-pattern of some of the veneers. Current price, the suite: $400–$700. (Credit: *Maine Antique Digest*)

Figure 85

Above: A Waterfall sideboard. The heavy look in furniture made a comeback with these designs. Current price: $150–$250.

Figure 86

Left: A Waterfall dining table. Current price: $150–$250.

More often than not, Depression Modern furniture is sturdy stuff. You'll find it both in individual pieces and in suites, especially those for the bedroom and dining room.

Some Depression Modern, like the ubiquitous Waterfall furniture, is veneered, but the veneers are almost always attached firmly with strong glues. On the other hand, and as I've already mentioned, much Depression Modern furniture is made of solid, standard cabinet woods like maple and oak, and the finishes are almost always found in good condition. If necessary, it's quite easy to change the color of this usually blonde furniture because the wood itself was originally bleached. I can't recommend this practice, however, because Depression Modern is on the brink of becoming very collectible. At

The Current Market

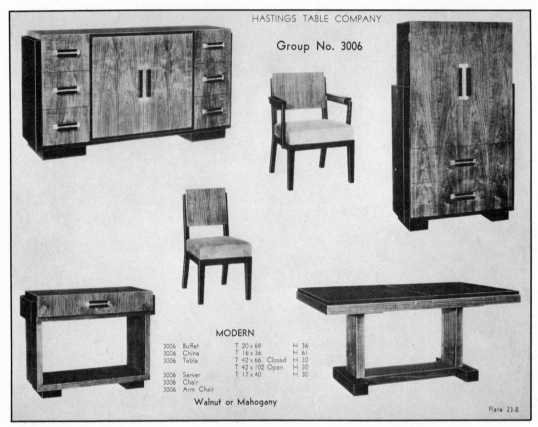

Figure 87

Not all Depression Modern furniture has rounded corners, as this walnut-veneered dining-room group from a Hastings Table Company catalog shows. Current prices: buffet, $150–$250; china closet, $150–$250; table, $175–$275; armchair, $75–$150; side chair, $50–$100.

present there is a growing market for it, especially in eastern urban areas. If its rediscovery is not simply a passing fad—and I don't think it is—then it would be far better to keep it in its original finish whenever possible. Since Depression Modern is popular in large cities (where it's often called Art Deco), the best place to buy it is anywhere *but* large cities. This furniture should become increasingly valuable as time goes by, if only because it is so distinctly and forthrightly American.

Regarding Art Deco and other modernistic furniture, it's not nearly as easy to find as Depression Modern, and when you do find it, it's likely to be relatively expensive —especially in cities, where it, too, is experiencing a rebirth. Frankly, I don't think the market for it will ever be particularly large. It's simply too idiosyncratic to appeal to large numbers of used-furniture buyers. Still, its rarity may tend to keep its price moving up.

12

—————❦—————

WELL-OILED EFFICIENCY:
SWEDISH MODERN, 1937–60 AND BEYOND

AS I MENTIONED in the previous chapter, Swedish Modern furniture had been shown to the world as early as the 1925 Paris expo at the Swedish pavilion—furniture designed by one Carl Malmsten. At that time Americans were not particularly taken with it. Today, however, the basic look not only survives but thrives. In fact, it promises to be one of the longest-lived styles that has ever been produced, at least in wooden case-piece furniture.

In spite of its early introduction in Paris, it was not until 1937 that the John Widdicomb Company of Grand Rapids introduced its own line of Swedish Modern—designed by one Carl Malmsten. Quite possibly the ultimate acceptance of the Swedish look had been conditioned by the earlier popularity of blonde American Modern furniture designed by Russel Wright. In any case, by 1939 Swedish Modern had become the undisputed star of the New York World's Fair.

The Historical Background

In order to achieve the Swedish look in the forties and fifties, some American manufacturers imported their own Scandinavian designers to create their new lines. What they and others came up with were functional, uncluttered designs: quiet expanses of light-colored woods with a well-oiled finish, delicately tapering legs with rounded contours, drawer handles that were sometimes recessed, mirrors that were often unframed, and beds with squared-off headboards that had built-in bookcases or

Figure 88

Classic international-style Swedish Modern furniture designed by Finn Juhl for the Baker Furniture Company in the 1950s. Current prices: table, $100–$200; chairs, $40–$60.

storage areas. It was a style that no one could passionately hate but that no one could passionately love, either. It impressed one with its obvious good taste, reliability, efficiency, and rational elegance. Rather than loving it, one simply admired it.

At its best, that is, for the basic Swedish look was quite easy to imitate with sleazy materials. At its worst, it was the most depressing stuff imaginable—the furniture of cheap motel rooms with paper-thin walls. Perhaps you know what I mean.

Figure 89

An American version of 1950s Swedish Modern that departs from the original designs, especially in the squarishness of the legs. Current price: $50–$75.

Figure 90

A 1950s bedroom furnished with Henredon Furniture Industries' concept of Swedish Modern. Current price, the suite: $150–$250.

Figure 91

More Finn Juhl designs. Current prices: three-piece vanity unit, $125–$225; table, $50–$75; bench, $30–$50; bed, $100–$200.

24½
Case
W. 36 D. 18 H. 30
Walnut
Note: 24-1 Same Case of Teak

20½
Powder Unit
W. 36 D. 22 H. 24
Walnut
Note: 20-1 Same Case of Teak

22½
Case
W. 36 D. 18 H. 30
Walnut
Note: 22-1 Same Case of Teak

9½ **Corner Shelf**
18 x 18 — Walnut
Fitted with Angle Irons for Suspending on Wall

523
Table
Top Closed 19 x 24 H. 20
Top Open 19 x 44 H. 20
Walnut and Maple

404
Bench
W. 26 D. 16½ H. 17½
Walnut and Maple

626
Bed
Headboard H. 31½
Footboard H. 21½
Twin or Full Size
Walnut and Maple

Figure 92

The basic Swedish Modern look persists in the 1980s, as this sideboard and hanging cupboard produced by the Winterhouse Furniture Company demonstrate. Although both pieces are totally squared off and thoroughly contemporary, the oil-finished walnut-veneer surfaces hark back to the 1950s, even to the 1930s (see figure 87). The chrome-and-leather chairs are Bauhaus inspired.

The Current Market

You'll find good American versions of Swedish Modern furniture made with one or more of such woods as walnut, teak, sycamore, maple, and birch. When pieces are veneered, great care will have been taken to match the veneers and to finish them in mellow, natural tones. You may also find good furniture that resembles Swedish or Danish Modern in finish but that somehow looks different: perhaps the legs aren't tapered or the cases have rhomboid rather than square shapes. This variation on Swedish will simply have been an attempt by the manufacturer to create its own concept of a very modern line. And I've already mentioned that some Swedish Modern is very cheaply made. One instant visual tip-off to this poorer quality furniture is that it's often finished far more darkly than the classic Swedish Modern—usually an attempt to hide the wood.

I doubt whether mass-produced Swedish Modern will ever be considered a style of furniture that's worth collecting, like Golden Oak or even Depression Modern. First, it's too international in style, not distinctly American enough to merit the collector's attention. Second, it's too easily associated with office furniture, where its implicit efficiency works perfectly, of course, but where one is called on more to ignore it than to warm up to it.

On the other hand, though somewhat cool and aloof, Swedish Modern is not nearly as icy as Bauhaus-inspired chrome and leather and glass and bent-plywood furniture. Swedish does retain the warm look of good woods, which can be quite beautiful, especially in walnut or teak. The best designer pieces were originally quite expensive, and at used-furniture prices, therefore, can be a real bargain. Furthermore, some of the earlier American designs do look "dated" enough to announce clearly the era in which they were made. Whether or not those earlier designs in good woods will become a worthwhile investment, however, remains to be seen. At this writing, they're not.

13

---❖---

SPECIALTY FURNITURE:
BENTWOOD, METAL, WICKER, AND HORN

WHAT IS SPECIAL ABOUT specialty furniture is that it's made in shapes or from materials that set it apart from the crowd. Since furniture can be made from almost anything and in almost any shape—and probably has been—I'm not going to attempt to cover all specialty furniture in this one chapter. The following, then, are a few of the more available items you're likely to find, that might fit your budget.

Bentwood Furniture

This interesting and popular furniture is associated in most people's minds with Austrian manufacturer Michael Thonet. Almost everyone is familiar with his famous, curvacious bentwood rocker and his Vienna cafe chair. Indeed, chairs are the form that is most amenable to bentwood construction, and so that's what you'll find in the marketplace.

Thonet first manufactured bentwood furniture about 1840. In 1856 he perfected his techniques for bending Carpathian beechwood. Finally, in 1876, he began production of the first Vienna cafe chairs, which must be one of the most continuously popular designs ever made; his company to date has sold over fifty million units and is still going strong.

Thonet's genius was not only in design and bending techniques but also in construction, for bentwood furniture is not permanently joined but only screwed together.

Figure 93

A pair of bent-steel lawn chairs, made in imitation of bentwood furniture. The seats have water-drainage holes. Current price, the pair: $50–$100.

Figure 94

A Thonet-style bentwood rocker is shown in the foreground of this otherwise contemporary den. Bentwood furniture seems to complement virtually every other style. Note the "neo-Art Nouveau" end table, based on designs by Eero Saarinen from the 1950s. Current price, the bentwood rocker: $200–$350.

Figure 95

An unusual bentwood settee. Note the screws holding the piece together. Current price: $125–$225.

It could be exported unassembled and then put together by the distributor. Nonetheless, bentwood furniture is sturdy. Eventually it was manufactured in various European countries and in America and sold in different varnished finishes, the most common being mahogany, walnut, and ebony. The seats were either thin plywood or cane, and both versions may be found broken beyond repair. The cane is relatively easy to replace with machine-caning made in sheets, and the plywood can be replaced as well. But I don't recommend the latter since the new seats never quite catch the slightly curved, patterned look of the originals.

Bentwood furniture is usually reasonably priced, and authentic Thonet labels are not as difficult to find as you might think.

Figure 96

A selection of brass-bed designs from turn-of-the-century mail-order catalog. Current price: $400–$750.

Metal Furniture

Brass Beds. Good solid-brass beds actually have a cast-iron core that is wrapped with brass tubing. The finials, however, have no core, and so you can check them with a magnet to determine whether or not they are solid brass as opposed to plated. (Remember that solid brass is not magnetic.) Also, you should be able to locate a seam along each long brass tube.

The earlier brass beds were not made in the modern queen and king sizes. The patterns of brasswork on these beds range from a fairly straightforward cannonball shape to a multitude of vertical tubes and bentwork. These beds were originally coated with lacquer to preserve their finish, and used beds will probably have to be stripped, polished, and relacquered. Solid-brass beds were comparatively expensive when they were first sold, and today the early ones may be astronomically expensive. The later beds with square tubing—often called Mission beds be-

Figure 97

An advertisement for an Art Nouveau iron bed. Current price: $200–$300. (*The Grand Rapids Furniture Record,* 1901)

Figure 98

Two ornate iron beds from a turn-of-the-century mail-order catalog. Note the difference in original price between these and the brass beds in figure 96. Current price: $200–$300.

cause of their geometricality—will be much less costly but also may be plated rather than solid.

Iron beds. These were for people who couldn't afford brass beds, the most expensive iron models originally costing only about one third as much as a brass model. They were usually enameled in solid white, but multicolored beds can also be found in combinations of white and maroon, light blue, and light green. Gold beds, made to imitate brass, were also sold. The best iron beds have lots of solid-brass trim—vases, rosettes, and finials, for example. Those are the ones I recommend buying, since the totally plain models will never be worth much.

Steel Beds. Enameled in wood grains or solid colors and often decorated with painted patterns and steel "cane-work," steel beds with rounded contours were popular in

Figure 99

A steel-bed outfit advertised in a 1931 mail-order catalog. Note the Art Deco design on the head- and footboards. Current price, bed only: $50–$100.

the twenties and thirties. The better ones have two-inch-diameter outer posts with ridges that imitate molding, as opposed to their being simply round. The baked finishes are generally easy to clean and won't chip or crack unless they're abused.

Iron Lawn Furniture. Cast-iron lawn furniture—sometimes called cemetery furniture—was made in a wide variety of patterns, usually with floral motifs and painted white or dark green. It's heavy and uncomfortable but attractive. It may also be very expensive since it's in demand. The original castings were quite well defined; beware of reproductions newly cast from old molds, which will appear less sharp than the originals. Rusty bare spots on this furniture should be primed and painted with rust-proof products.

Figure 100

A handsome set of wire lawn furniture. Current price, the set: $200
–$300.

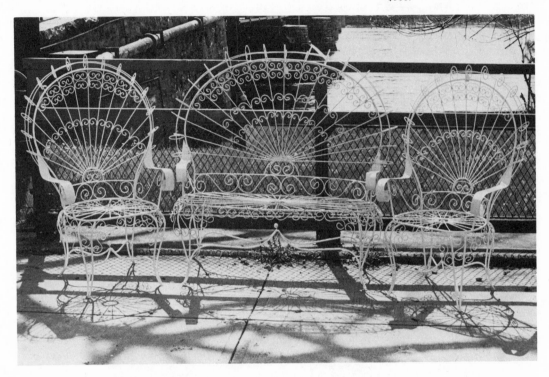

Wire Lawn Furniture. The same iron used for cast-iron furniture was extruded to form wire, which was then bent into curlicues and furbelows to form the intricate patterns of wire lawn furniture. It's much less fragile than it looks, but rust can be a serious problem, weakening sections of the furniture until it simply gives way. Therefore you should check this furniture carefully before buying it to assure yourself that new paint isn't hiding weakened sections.

Wicker Furniture

Wicker is a generic term that covers furniture made from all sorts of materials—prairie grass, rattan, cane, rush, and man-made paper rush.

The earliest pieces, circa 1850–90, were tightly woven by hand around hardwood frames, then painted or left natural. This early, unpainted wicker furniture is prized

Figure 101

Prairie-grass furniture. Current prices: chaise longue, $250–$450; chair, $125–$175; plant stand, $75 –$100. (*The Grand Rapids Furniture Record,* 1901)

Figure 102

An excellent, naturally finished wicker rocking chair from about 1900. Current price: $175–$225.

Figure 103

Above: A good wicker armchair from about 1900. Note how the new white paint has not clogged the wickerwork. Current price: $125–$175.

Figure 104

Left: A loom-woven wicker chair on a metal frame from the 1930s. Current price: $75–$125.

Figure 105

Multicolored paper-rush designs shown in a 1930s mail-order catalog. Current prices: couch, $200–$300; chair, $75–$125; planter, $75–$100; table, $75–$100.

by collectors. Around 1900 less expensive pieces were made with an open weave that not only required less material but less workmanship. In 1917 a mechanical loom was invented that could weave paper rush, and furniture made of that was even cheaper than the open-weave variety. The paper for this furniture was often dyed before being woven, and then the completed pieces were varnished. Elaborate color schemes were often used, and it can be found in up to four different hues, shading from one to the next. The frames were generally of metal rather than wood.

Originally made for the porch or lawn, wicker eventually moved inside. As a 1920s advertisement for the Karpen Furniture Company smoothly put it, "Every homemaker covets its informal charm for at least one room. It invites new and interesting schemes for the sun room, living room, breakfast room, and bed room. To summer homes and cottages it brings a cool and airy comfort." Be that as it may, by the mid-1930s wicker was out of fashion.

Today, of course, just the opposite is true. And because

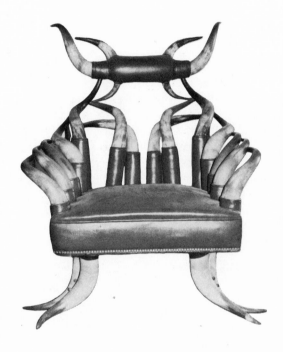

Figure 106

It's a good horn-chair, but please don't stumble into it in the dark! Current price: $400–$600.

of wicker's versatility, you'll find it in an astonishing array of forms—not only chairs, sofas, and tables, but desks, beds, plant stands, whatnot shelves, tea carts, lamps, bookshelves, clothes trees, phonograph cabinets, and more.

Don't buy wicker furniture that is rotted, either in the wickerwork itself or in the hardwood frame. Broken hardwood frames should also be avoided since the only way to repair them is to remove the wicker. On the other hand, wickerwork that is simply broken can be easily repaired with more wicker and white glue; some of the pros also use wire. Wicker can also be stripped in a cold tank of layers of paint that clog the reeds. (See the "Further Reading" section for a good book on the subject of repairs.)

Horn Furniture

Made in part of steer, buffalo, or elk horns and upholstered in fabric or leather, horn furniture has got to be some of the most bizarre stuff ever made. I put it in a class with armadillo nut-baskets and elephant-foot wastebaskets. But Abe Lincoln and Teddy Roosevelt apparently owned a few pieces of it, some collectors love it, and I'm sure no self-respecting bullfighter would be without it, so perhaps the fact that horn furniture makes me nervous is my problem. It was made from about 1860 to just before World War I, often by hand. If you like it, more power to you, but be aware that horn furniture can be very expensive, single pieces selling for more than a thousand dollars, especially in the Southwest.

APPENDIX:
A USED-FURNITURE CHRONOLOGY

1819 Birth of John Ruskin

1825 Erie Canal opens; beginning of westward migration of manufacturing

1834 Birth of William Morris

1836 Birth of Charles Lock Eastlake

ca 1840 Michael Thonet begins production of bentwood furniture in Vienna, Austria

1848 Birth of Louis C. Tiffany

1850s Parlor and bedroom furniture first sold in matching suites

Railroads begin to erode advantages of long-haul freight on the Erie Canal

Handmade furniture production in America almost nonexistent

1851 Crystal Palace Exposition, London (first international exhibition of fine, industrial, and decorative arts)

1856 Birth of Elbert Hubbard

1858 Birth of Gustav Stickley

1862 Founding of Morris and Company, London

1865 First American patent issued for plywood

1866 Morris and Company introduces adjustable-back "Morris" chair

Transatlantic telegraph cable completed

1867 First Paris international exposition

1869 Transcontinental railroad completed

ca 1870 Invention of the cane-weaving loom for chair seats

1872 First American publication of Eastlake's *Hints on Household Taste*

Montgomery Ward and Company issues its first mail-order catalog

1876 Centennial Exposition, Philadelphia; Eastlake and British styles predominate, as well as oriental

Thonet begins production of the Vienna cafe chair

1877 Widdicomb Furniture Company, Grand Rapids, issues the first illustrated American furniture catalog

1878 First official Grand Rapids Furniture Market

1879 Founding of the firm of Louis C. Tiffany and Company, Associated Artists

1881 World's first central electric-light power plant opens, New York City

1883 First skyscraper built in Chicago

1886 Stickley begins production of Arts and Crafts furniture

1889 Paris international exposition; Art Nouveau shown

1890s Twin beds introduced because sleeping alone is thought to be more "sanitary"

1891 A. C. Roebuck Company issues its first catalog

1893 World's Columbian Exposition, Chicago; Grand Rapids Chair Company shows an asymmetrical side-by-side secretary bookcase
First catalog issued by Sears, Roebuck and Company

1895 Hubbard establishes his Roycroft Shops in East Aurora, New York
Samuel Bing opens his Salon de L'Art Nouveau in Paris
Guglielmo Marconi first demonstrates the "wireless"

1896 Death of Morris

1898 Stickley establishes his Craftsman Workshops in Eastwood, New York

1900 Paris international exposition; Art Nouveau shown in many variations; John Widdicomb Company wins a gold medal for a bedroom suite
Stickley's Craftsman Furniture shown at semiannual market in Grand Rapids
Death of John Ruskin

ca 1900 Introduction of "unit," or "sectional," furniture, an American invention first used in bookcases

1901 Pan-American Exposition, Buffalo, New York; Arts and Crafts Movement production strong
Stickley's *The Craftsman* magazine first published

1902 Turin (Italy) exposition; Mission and Art Nouveau shown

1903 Wright Brothers make first sustained airplane flight

1904 Louisiana Purchase Exposition, St. Louis
Introduction of fiber reed (paper) for wicker furniture

1906 Death of Eastlake

1908 Model T Ford introduced

1915 Stickley goes bankrupt
Hubbard dies on the *Lusitania*

1916 *The Craftsman* magazine ceases publication
U.S. tariff regulations define antiques as objects of esthetic merit made before 1830

1917– 1940 Fifteen exhibitions of American Industrial Art held at the Metropolitan Museum, New York

1919 Bauhaus founded by Walter Gropius, Weimar, Germany

1920 First commercial radio station licensed in U.S. (KDKA, Pittsburgh)

1922 Discovery of the tomb of Tutankhamen near Luxor, Egypt

1925 *Exposition Internationale des Arts Décoratifs et Industriels Modernes* in Paris; Art Deco shown; U.S. not represented

1927 Macy's, New York, sponsors an exhibition of "New Art"

1928 Macy's sponsors its International Exhibition of Art and Industry; other stores with similar exhibits include B. Altman and Lord and Taylor

1929 Founding of the Museum of Modern Art, New York

1930s Interior decoration and industrial design become established professions in America

1933 Bauhaus closed by the Nazis; designers find refuge in the U.S.
Death of Tiffany

1933– 1934 Century of Progress Exposition, Chicago; Modern furniture shown; introduction of modular furniture

1935 Conant-Ball Company, Gardner, Massachusetts, introduces American Modern line designed by Russel Wright

1937 Swedish Modern furniture line introduced by John Widdicomb Company

ca Synthetic resin glues become available from Germany; combined with the hot-plate press, they revolutionize veneering and plywood production in the 1940s

1938 Introduction of Waterfall furniture in America

1939– New York World's Fair; Swedish
1940 Modern predominates Golden Gate International Exposition, San Francisco

1942 Death of Stickley

1943– Wernher von Braun develops first
1944 liquid-fuel rockets in Germany

1950s International Style begins to dominate decorative arts

1957 Sputnik launched by U.S.S.R.

1958 Brussels World's Fair

1961 First man launched into Earth orbit by U.S.S.R.

1962 Century 21 Exposition, Seattle
First transatlantic television broadcast via satellite

1964– New York World's Fair
1965

1966 U.S. tariff regulations redefine antiques as objects made prior to one hundred years before their date of entry into the U.S.

FURTHER READING

Battersby, Martin. *The Decorative Thirties.* New York: Walker and Company, 1971.

Boger, Louise Ade. *The Complete Guide to Furniture Styles.* New York: Scribner's, 1969 (enlarged edition).

Brady, Nancy Hubbard (ed.). *Roycroft Handmade Furniture: A Facsimile of a 1912 Catalogue.* East Aurora, New York: House of Hubbard, 1973.

Butler, Joseph T. *American Furniture.* London: Triune Books, 1973.

Clark, Robert Judson, et al. *The Arts and Crafts Movement in America 1876–1916.* Princeton: Princeton University Press (distributor), 1972.

Comstock, Ruth B. *Cane Seats for Chairs* (Bulletin 681); *Splint Seats for Chairs* (Bulletin 682); *Rush Seats for Chairs* (Bulletin 683). Ithaca, New York: Cornell University College of Human Ecology (Ithaca, New York 14853), 1976 (revised editions).

Constantine, Albert, Jr., and Harry J. Hobbs. *Know Your Woods.* New York: Scribner's, 1975.

Davidson, Marshall B. (ed.). *The American Heritage History of Antiques from the Civil War to World War I.* American Heritage Publishing Company, 1969.

Eastlake, Charles Lock. *Hints on Household Taste in Furniture, Upholstery and Other Details.* New York: Dover, 1969 (facsimile of 1878 edition).

Freeman, John Crosby. *Forgotten Rebel: Gustav Stickley and His Craftsman Mission Furniture.* Watkins Glen, New York: Century, 1966.

Gowans, Alan. *Images of American Living: Four Centuries of Architecture and Furniture as Cultural Expression.* Philadelphia: Lippincott, 1964.

Greif, Martin. *Depression Modern: The Thirties Style in America.* New York: Universe, 1975.

Grotz, George. *The New Antiques: Knowing and Buying Victorian Furniture.* Garden City, New York: Doubleday, 1964.

Lynes, Russell. *The Tastemakers.* New York: Harper and Brothers, 1954.

Rodd, John. *Restoring and Repairing Antique Furniture.* New York: Van Nostrand, 1976.

Saunders, Richard. *Collecting and Restoring Wicker Furniture.* New York: Crown, 1976.

Semple, Marlene. *Introductory Guide to Midwest Antiques.* Matteson, Illinois: Greatlakes Living Press, 1976.

Sloan, Eric. *A Reverence for Wood.* New York: Ballantine Books, 1973 (paperback).

United States Department of Agriculture, Forest Service. *Wood: Colors and Kinds* (Agriculture Handbook 101). Washington, D.C.: U.S. Government Printing Office, 1956.

INDEX

3.6.2